Teachers' Rights and Liabilities under the Law

This publication is designed to provide accurate and authoritative information in regard to the subject matter covered. It is sold with the understanding that the publisher is not engaged in rendering legal, accounting or other professional service. If legal advice or other expert assistance is required, the services of a competent professional person should be sought.

Teachers' Rights and Liabilities under the Law

Laurence Kallen, J. D.

Illustrations by Enid Warner Romanek

New York

To my wife Bonnie, who has a lot of patience,
and to my friend Howard Robinson, who has
big ideas.

Published by ARCO PUBLISHING COMPANY, INC.
219 Park Avenue South, New York, N.Y. 10003

Copyright © Laurence H. Kallen, 1971

All Rights Reserved

Library of Congress Catalog Number 76-161212

ISBN 0-668-02498-4

Printed in the United States of America

Contents

III. THE TEACHER'S RIGHTS

EPILOGUE

APPENDICES

1

This Book—What and Why

IT is not fun to be sued. If you live in one of those states where the boards of education are required to pay pupils' damage awards, or if you have professional insurance, you may never suffer the staggering financial consequences which may result from the successful suit by an injured pupil against his teacher. Nevertheless, a teacher who is being sued "pays" with many hours of worry and inconvenience, and damage to his reputation—these are costs which cannot be recouped. The only way to really win a lawsuit is . . . not to be sued at all!

This handbook is intended to provide an "ounce of prevention." That is, its value lies in sensitizing the reader to the legal danger areas and suggesting the way in which the courts have approached such problems, so that the teacher (and the principal, who under the law is merely the "head teacher") may plan his activities in a manner which minimizes the chances of legal liability. It is most emphatically *not* designed to provide legal representation in the event a suit against the teacher is filed or seems imminent. Consulting this book at such a time is a useless activity—at that point the teacher needs a good lawyer to help protect his interests, not a book to tell him what he should have done. *The teacher who becomes the subject of a lawsuit should immediately contact a lawyer.* Since this book contains information as to general principles of law in such areas as negligence, assault and battery, and defamation, as well as detailed answers concerning the various aspects of the teacher-pupil relationship, it is suggested that the teacher read it from cover to cover at the outset. In this fashion not only will the teacher's specific questions be answered, but also he will recognize the existence of a general framework within which he should approach new problems.

Further, this handbook is not intended to provide advice concerning the *best* ways of handling pupils or teaching in a classroom. It is the province of professional ethics and educational theory to suggest to the teacher what he should do to provide the best possible education for his pupils; and legal do's and don'ts merely describe the minimum which a teacher must do and the maximum which he may do without incurring monetary loss. It is for this reason that your local school board may require more strict standards than the legal strictures named in this book.

The information and advice offered here are based upon the study of the statutes and judicial decisions of all fifty states and the District of Columbia, and are presented in such a manner that the reader will know where his state stands on each rule of law. On most issues there have been several key cases, scattered amongst the states. Where the decisions have agreed on an issue and the reasoning in them is sound, it will be assumed that the rule applies even in those states whose courts have not yet been presented with the problem. While courts are only bound by previous decisions within their state, decisions in other states are highly persuasive and will be followed if they are well reasoned. Conversely, where the courts in different states have differed on an issue, the reader will be informed as to where his state stands. On certain issues—corporal punishment, for example—many states have enacted statutes. Since *statutes apply only to the state in which enacted,* there may be many differences among the states which will be duly noted for the reader.

Each and every statement in this book regarding the legal limits of the teacher's rights and duties is supported by specific statutory and/or judicial authority. It was felt that to include hundreds of footnote numbers in the text would be too distracting; therefore legal support for statements in the text will be found, listed by page number and catch-phrase, in APPENDIX B. Thus, if the teacher reads on page 2 that "It is negligent for the teacher to be stationed in the building while the children are on the playground," he may assume that such a statement is supported by legal authority. However, if he wishes to find out more about the type of legal support for the statement, he may turn to APPENDIX B and, under *page 7* "May not supervise playground activities while in building," he will see *"Lopez,"* which is the plaintiff's name in the case that decided the issue. (Statutes will be fully cited in APPENDIX B, while cases will be cited by plaintiff's name.) To get the complete citation for any case, the reader may look it up in *"Cases Cited,"* APPENDIX C. "Cf.," preceding a case citation indicates that the cited decision ruled upon an issue is not exactly the same as the one being discussed in the text, but such similar principles were involved in the cited case that it provides a useful clue as to how courts would rule on the point.

In the "Cases Cited" appendix, most citations to cases name two sources where the teacher may go to find the printed opinion, as well as the date of the decision. The first source listed names the volume of the state reporter in which the opinion may be found; the second names the volume of the West Publishing Company's Regional *Reporter*—whether it be Atlantic (A.), Northeast (N.E.), Northwest (N.W.), Pacific (P.), Southeastern (S.E.), Southern (So.), or Southwestern (S.W.) —in which it also appears. For example, 237 Mich. 603, 213 N.W. 172 (1927), refers to a 1927 decision which may be found either on page 603 of volume 237 of the cases published by the state of Michigan, or on page 172 of volume 213 of West's Northwestern *Reporter*. (Recent cases may appear in the second series of the *Reporters*—for example, 330 S.W. 2d 708.) Some cases are from states which do not print state reporters and so may be found only in the relevant Regional *Reporter*, while certain older decisions predate the establishment of the Regional *Reporters* and are thus only reported in the compilations put out by the state. A quote is cited according to the page in the Regional *Reporter* in which it may be found in the Regional *Reporters,* those of California and New official reporter—for example, 393 U.S. 503; federal trial court decisions are reported in the Federal Supplement (F.S.), and federal Court of Appeals cases are printed in the Federal Reporter (F.). Some states have a system of appeals courts to which a party usually must appeal before reaching the state supreme court. Decisions of these courts are usually printed in separate state reporters (for example, 117 Mich. App. 238). Although the appeals courts' decisions of most states are also found in the Regional *Reporters,* those of California and New York (the two most litigious states) rate their own West *Reporters,* the California *Reporter* (Cal. Rptr.) and the New York *Supplement* (N.Y.S.).

Every state has an Attorney General, who is the state's chief lawyer. Government employees may write him and request his advice concerning their duties, and the opinions are made public and published. As such, the Attorney General's opinions have no force of law and are not binding upon either courts or citizens; however, they are important sources in that they are persuasive when cited to courts and contain clues as to proper legal reasoning on issues which have not yet been litigated.

I

Negligence Law and the Teacher

2

The Elements of a Lawsuit for Negligence

THIS chapter will provide the foundation upon which later chapters will build since it will outline the basic principles and approaches of general negligence law. Although the reader may find this chapter rather "heavy," if the teacher can get a feel for the general principles he will have no trouble at all seeing the patterns inherent in the later chapters dealing with school law, since teacher-liability issues are but specific applications of the abstract principles of negligence law.

Every person in our society has the duty to organize his daily activities in a manner which will not subject others to an unreasonable risk of harm: that is, every person must estimate the chances that some injury will result from his act as well as the seriousness of the harm that is likely to come about if there is an injury, and must avoid those activities which society feels produce too great a risk. It is the jury who measures the person's act against the standard of behavior required by our society. If the act is found to be below the standard, the actor will be required to pay for any injury which his act has occasioned.

The jury is guided by certain legal principles in determining whether an act has met the standard of conduct set by society, and the plaintiff must show why, in light of the legal principles, the defendant should be made to pay for the plaintiff's injuries.

13

Therefore, the best way to discuss the legal principles concerned with finding the standard of care is to look at those elements which the pupil-plaintiff must prove to the satisfaction of the jury if he is to be entitled to recover damages from the teacher-defendant.

A finding of negligence in a court of law must be based upon the proof of four elements. If the pupil fails to prove any one of these elements, he will not be able to recover from the teacher. The pupil must prove:

1) a *duty* on the part of the teacher to not subject the pupil to an unreasonable risk of harm;

2) a *negligent act or omission*—an act or failure to act which a reasonable teacher, under the circumstances, ought to have foreseen would subject the pupil to an unreasonable risk of harm;

3) *injury* or damage to the pupil's person or property;

4) a sufficiently *close connection between the negligent act or omission and the injury* to warrant making the teacher pay for it—a finding of "proximate cause."

Duty

The pupil-plaintiff must show that the relationship between him and the teacher-defendant was sufficiently close so that the teacher was under a legal obligation not to subject the pupil to an unreasonable risk of harm.

Even in non-teacher cases, it will nearly always be found that a duty existed in those negligence cases where defendant's *act* produced the injury, since acts must be carefully regulated in a busy, complex society in order to reduce the hazards of living at such a pace. Where defendant's *failure to act* is at issue it often may be found that no duty to act existed, since, in general, there is no duty (and often no right) in our society for persons to become involved in other people's affairs. Thus a doctor has no duty to render first aid if he comes upon an accident scene, and a person has no duty to attempt to rescue a drowning man. However, since this is a harsh rule, the courts have decided that an affirmative duty to act may be imposed where defendant has accepted any responsibility for the safe-keeping of plaintiff; it is into this category that the teacher-pupil relationship falls.

It is unlikely that a pupil ever could fail to show that a teacher owed him a duty of due care, since teachers are part of an institution—the school system—which assumes control over children for a large part of the day. That is, since children are deprived of the protection of their parents during that part of the day when they are being cared for by the schools, the school personnel must accept responsibility for their safety. Thus teachers not only may be found negligent for doing unreasonably dangerous acts, but they also may be held liable for failure to act. For example, they must supervise pupils' activities, warn them of dangers, protect them from themselves and each other, disarm them, stop fights, and summon first aid—duties which they are not required to exercise towards members of the general public who are not under their protection.

Negligent Act or Omission

The pupil-plaintiff must prove that the teacher-defendant breached his duty of due care by subjecting the pupil to an un-reasonable risk of harm. A teacher is not held liable merely because an accident occurred; it must be proved that a reasonably prudent person in the defendant-teacher's shoes would have foreseen the injury and would have acted to prevent it. It is the jury who decides what a "reasonably prudent person" would have "foreseen."

The concept of a "reasonably prudent person" permeates negligence law. He is not the "average" person, who sometimes makes mistakes, but rather he is the perfect ideal; he is that perfect citizen whose behavior is *always* equal to that required by society. He always acts with due care for his safety and for the safety of others: he always watches where he is going, never drives too fast for conditions, and always takes reasonable precautions to protect the safety of those under his care.

When the jury compares the actions of a defendant to those of a reasonably prudent person, that "ideal citizen" is placed into the situation as it existed at the time of the acts, and is given the same physical characteristics and special skills as the actual defendant. To take an extreme example, a crippled man with an extensive knowledge of first aid is held to the standard of care of a reasonably prudent crippled man with an extensive knowledge of first aid, placed in similar circumstances. However, although special skills and physical characteristics are taken into account, no allowances are made for the lack of intelligence or quick temper of the adult defendant (probably because they are too hard to discern and measure)—he is held to the standard of a reasonably prudent person of average intelligence and even temperament. Further, he cannot claim to possess less knowledge about ordinary matters than the ordinary person.

Since the reasonably prudent person is, in effect, placed in the defendant's shoes, the teacher being sued by a pupil is held to that standard of care which an ideal teacher would have exercised, and the jury will take into account those particular responsibilities which teachers have towards pupils.

In addition, it is up to the jury to determine whether that reasonably prudent teacher would have *foreseen* that his act or omission exposed the pupil to an unreasonable risk of harm. To be foreseeable, it is not necessary that the exact course of the accident or the exact type of injury be predictable.

> "The law does not require precision in foreseeing the exact hazard or consequence which happens. It is sufficient if what occurred was one of the kind of consequences which might reasonably be foreseen. *Comstock v. General Motors Corp.*"

Thus a teacher only need realize that some kind of harm is likely to come from a flipped jackknife, a hot bowl of soup placed near a two-year old, a dark coatroom, inadequate playground supervision, a pencil thrown by the teacher, or an easily-upset upright piano turned with the keyboard towards the wall, in order to require that teacher to alleviate the danger. On the other hand, where the risk would have been completely unforeseeable to a reasonably prudent teacher, or the chances of injury would have been so small that, in light of the seriousness of the possible injury, it would not be reasonable to require a teacher to take precautions against it, then any adverse result is an "unavoidable accident" for which no one will be held liable.

>The plaintiff in the case of *Wire* v. *Williams* was injured while jumping rope on the playground. The teacher was holding one end of the rope, and when the pupil stepped on the rope it flew out of the teacher's hands and hit the student in the teeth.
>
>After hearing all the evidence, the trial court did not allow the case to go to the jury but rather ruled that, as a matter of law, the teacher was not negligent. The pupil appealed.
>
>The Minnesota Supreme Court affirmed the trial judge's decision. The Court ruled that, although teachers owe a duty of care to students, it was not legally "foreseeable" that the teacher's acts would result in injury.

It is not often easy to predict whether a teacher will be held liable, since juries' determinations of "foreseeability" often are based more upon who the jury feels should bear the loss than upon the actual predictability of the injury. For example, although it has been acknowledged that the presence of children in any situation makes the chances of injury more likely due to their inquisitiveness and lack of mature judgment, one Michigan case held that it was not "foreseeable" that a pupil who was allowed to stand upon a chair in order to water plants with a glass bottle would fall and cut herself. On the other hand, it has been deemed "foreseeable" that a pupil would develop heart trouble carrying books to a stockroom. This is not to say that the teacher should despair at trying to define his area of responsibility, but rather that he should develop an awareness of the trouble areas and should go to great lengths to take precautions; such added caution will serve to head off lawsuits before they start and will prevent the teacher from being subjected to the deliberations of a jury.

Illinois and Texas are the only states in which the teacher is not held to the standard of reasonable care for all classroom activities. By statute, public employees in Illinois and Texas are not liable for mere negligence in the undertaking of "discretion-ary" acts. For those classroom decisions which require pro-fessional judgment (teaching methods, etc.), the teacher will not be liable unless he has acted with "willful and wanton negligence" —that is, with conscious disregard of a risk which threatens probable injury to a pupil. Put differently, to prove negligence a plaintiff must prove that the teacher was *unaware* of (did not foresee) a risk which a *reasonable* person would have avoided; to prove willful and wanton negligence a pupil must show that the teacher was *aware* of a danger which threatened *probable* injury, yet went ahead anyway. However, there is a problem for Illinois and Texas teachers: it is largely an open question as to which are "ministerial acts" measured by normal standards of negligence and which are "discretionary acts" subject only to the willful and wanton standard. One Illinois decision has ruled that the decision to allow an aggressive pupil to play on a bas-ketball team is discretionary, and another case decided similarly with regard to the amount of pupil movement permitted about the classroom. On the other extreme, only negligence need be proved where a chemistry instructor's experiment has ex-ploded. By its terms, the Texas statute does not provide "dis-cretionary act" protection for corporal punishment. The area in between is as yet undefined. Is it an act of discretion to allow pupils to play a dangerous game? fail to show up for playground duty? fail to enforce safety rules? authorize use of improper equipment? The lesson is obvious: the Illinois and Texas teacher would be wise to follow the guidelines concerning negligence so as to be sure of legal protection.

Injury

The third element of proof is a showing of actual damages; plaintiff must prove an actual injury to his person or property. It should be noted that if the defendant is found liable, not only must he pay for any injuries directly resulting from his wrongful acts, but he must also pay for any subsequent re-injury which was occasioned by the plaintiff's physical impairment, any diseases resulting from the plaintiff's lowered defenses, any harm received as the result of negligent medical treatment of the injury, and any further physical injuries caused by the emotional shock surrounding the injury.

Close Connection Between the Negligent Act or Omission and the Injury

The fourth element of proof on the part of the pupil-plaintiff involves showing to the jury that there was such a close connection between the teacher-defendant's negligence and the injury that defendant should be required to pay for it. This involves showing two things:

1) that the teacher's negligence was a "cause in fact"— the injury would not have occurred but for the teacher's negligent act or omission; and

2) that the teacher's negligence was a "proximate cause"—the connection between the negligent act or omission and the injury is sufficiently close so that it would be fair to require the teacher to pay for the pupil's injury.

If the pupil fails to prove either (1) or (2) he cannot recover from the teacher.

In order to determine whether the teacher's act was a cause in fact, the jury must consider whether the injury would have failed to occur had the negligent act or omission of the teacher not taken place. For example, it is a cause in fact that a train holds up a motorist at a railroad crossing for five minutes, where a tree later falls on the motorist's car as he is driving down the road; that is, but for the five minute wait plaintiff would have been five minutes farther down the road when the tree fell! (Remember, this alone is not sufficient to make the railroad liable. Cause in fact must still be coupled with the other elements of proof before liability is imposed.) Although the relation is obvious in most cases, in some cases defendant's act may turn out to not be a cause in fact. For example, it may be wrongful for a property owner to fail to repair a hole in a fence which is big enough for a child to slip through, but it will not result in liability where it can be shown that the injured child climbed *over* the fence. Although it may be a negligent omission for a teacher to fail to supervise pupils at play, the failure to do so will not result in liability where two boys bumped heads in the normal course of a basketball game.

In order to determine whether a teacher's negligence was a proximate cause of the injury, the jury must look to see whether the actions occurred in a natural and continuous sequence, unbroken by any new, independent cause, to produce the injury. If the jury finds that the negligence produced the injury in a natural and continuous sequence, a teacher will not escape liability merely because his negligence was not the last cause or merely because of a lapse of time between his act or omission and the injury. Two non-teacher cases may be taken as examples of this principle: a motorist was held liable when a canopy fell upon a person nine hours after that motorist had knocked the supporting pillars out from under it; and a lightning rod salesman was found liable for negligent installation when the house was struck by lightning seven years after installation.

The courts are often faced with the situation where there are two negligent causes in fact, and they must decide whether the second cause so changed the "natural and continuous sequence" that the first cause is no longer a proximate cause, or whether the second cause was part of the sequence of events set in motion by the first cause and so both parties may be found liable. The common situation occurs where one negligent act or omission creates a dangerous situation, and then a second person's negligent act or omission interacts with the situation to produce an injury to a third person.

Usually the act of A will remain a proximate cause in spite of the existence of a later negligent act by B, when A should have realized that B might so act, or a reasonable person would not regard B's act as highly extraordinary. This rule is extremely broad, and offers the original actor very little protection from liability. A good example is a recent Michigan case, where an auto manufacturer who sold a car with defective brakes was held liable when a person who was aware of the defect negligently forgot about it and ran into another person. Teachers, too, are bound by this rule, as where a negligent act or omission by a teacher creates a dangerous situation upon which a pupil later negligently acts to injure another pupil.

However, where the teacher's negligence involves *supervisory* duties, he has the benefit of a special rule for teachers which will protect him from liability in some situations.

The teacher will be held liable only where the lack of supervision resulted in a *continuing* dangerous situation, as where the teacher's absence led to rowdy and dangerous play or left pupils exposed to a dangerous condition on the grounds, under the theory that the teacher would have seen the dangerous situation and would have halted it before injury occurred. The teacher will not be held liable where the latter negligent act of the pupil was sudden and without warning; the courts have denied recovery on the basis that the teacher could not have prevented the injury anyway. Such reasoning does not stand up to rigorous analysis since it ignores the fact that the mere presence of the teacher is often enough to prevent even isolated mischievous acts, and so it must be concluded that the courts have made a conscious decision to bypass abstract logical arguments in favor of a policy decision to limit the teacher's liability in such situations. That is, even though the lack of supervision could be found to be a cause in fact, since the presence of the teacher would have deterred the act, the courts have refused to consider it a proximate cause where the act was sudden and impulsive. Since the teacher will be held liable where his absence resulted in a dangerous situation but will not be held liable where the injury was the result of an isolated act, it is a matter of chance whether the teacher will be held liable!

The teacher escaped liability in *Segerman* v. *Jones* only after appealing the case to the Maryland Supreme Court.

The accident serving as the basis of the suit occurred while the teacher was holding an exercise class. During a series of exercises the teacher cautioned the pupils not to move from their assigned places, and then left the room for approximately five minutes on school business. One of the pupils moved closer to the record player to hear better, and as he continued his exercises he accidently struck plaintiff's head with his feet. After hearing the evidence the trial court found against the teacher and in favor of the pupil.

On appeal, the Supreme Court of Maryland reversed the trial court's decision and found in favor of the teacher. The court ruled that although there was evidence that the pupil was a physically active child, there was no rowdyism in this particular situation. The fact that the pupil did the pushups incorrectly and caused the accident was to be considered a legally "unforeseeable" occurrence. Since teachers are not liable for every accident occurring in their absence, and since the accident was the result of a sudden act, the teacher would not be held liable.

A similar problem arises when a pupil *intentionally* takes advantage of the teacher's negligence to harm another person; here too, the courts have treated teacher supervision cases differently than non-teacher cases. In non-teacher cases, the general rule is that a negligent person is not held liable for damage caused by the later malicious or criminal act of someone else. For example, in one case a railroad was not held liable for the fire following their negligent derailment of a tank car, where that fire was maliciously started by a bystander. However, teachers who have failed to provide proper supervision *are* held liable for intentional injuries inflicted by their pupils which are not sudden, isolated acts, under the theory that the teacher would have stopped the assault had he been present. Therefore, a teacher may be held liable for injuries resulting from an attack upon a pupil, a fight, or even forcible rape, but will not be liable in those cases where the malicious act was sudden and without warning.

3

Defenses to a Suit for Negligence

IN general, there are four ways to defend a suit for negligence. The defendant may claim and prove:

1) defendant's immunity to suit; or
2) plaintiff's assumption of the risk which caused the injury; or
3) plaintiff's contributory negligence;
   or the defendant may:
4) prevent the plaintiff from proving any of the four elements of the plaintiff's case.

Under the common law, the various levels of government enjoy immunity from suit, but governmental employees (such as teachers) are not immune and may not claim the immunity of the state or municipal body. Thus in the majority of states the teacher will be the named defendant to a suit based upon negligence and will bear the burden of paying damages. In some states, however, the legislatures have provided that the school district will pay for damages done by its employees either by waiving its immunity to suit or by reimbursing the employee for any losses. Nevertheless, it must be remembered that even in those states where the teacher will not bear the monetary loss

23

it is the teacher whose acts will be questioned and whose reputation will be injured.

When defendant claims "assumption of risk," he is claiming that plaintiff recognized the degree of dangerousness in the situation, but went ahead and subjected himself to it anyway. Where plaintiff has voluntarily assumed the risk, the law will not make anyone else pay for the injury which has resulted. Although assumption of risk has been a traditional defense, it is so similar to contributory negligence that the following discussion of contributory negligence will apply equally to the assumption of risk defense.

By pleading the defense of "contributory negligence" the teacher claims that the pupil acted negligently toward his own safety, and so should not make anyone else pay for his injury. However, this defense has several defects for the teacher who wishes to utilize it.

Firstly, where there is a child plaintiff the judge will almost never rule that the child was contributorily negligent as a matter of law, and so at a minimum the teacher will be subjected to the painful and inconvenient trial process. This is because the child plaintiff is held only to the standard of a reasonable child of his age, capacity, and experience, and since so many factors must be taken into account it is almost always a jury question as to whether the child has met the necessary standard of care. In fact, the opposite is true: in many states judges will rule as a matter of law that very young children cannot be found contributorily negligent *under any circumstances.*

Secondly, in practice juries are not likely to hold even older children contributorily negligent because, very simply, they *expect* children to be heedless for their own safety. Thus, juries have found no contributory negligence where pupils have: jumped off bleachers, backed out of a door onto a driveway, run alongside a bus, dashed across a street, or attempted to cross a pit on a plank. Students who are learning the use of machines are expected to operate them imperfectly. There are other situations where it is likely that a jury will exonerate a pupil: where the teacher requested him to take part in the activity; the teacher has set a negligent example; the activity has been allowed to continue for so long that it is almost customary;

the teacher failed to instruct the pupil as to safety precautions; or the pupil was attracted to an interesting place or activity—those situations where the pupil's already weak sense of self-preservation was overpowered by the circumstances.

The teacher's main defense must be to prevent the plaintiff from proving the elements of his case. The best way to do this, of course, is to recognize the trouble areas and to take the precautionary steps which are indicated by the seriousness of the danger. If the teacher is aware of his safety responsibilities and is diligent in pursuing them, then he will have little to fear when an accident does occur.

It should be noted that it is no defense if the pupil's parent signed a note giving his permission for the child to take part in the activity, since the parent's consent is to the general activity, not to the negligence of the teacher. Even those notes which say that the parent waives any right to sue for negligence are of only limited usefulness; the pupil retains the right to sue for his injuries—a parent cannot sign away the rights of his child—and the teacher is insulated only against incidental damages.

II

The Teacher's Duties

4

Supervision on the School Grounds

Recess

SINCE recess is that time when youthful charges are released from the structured classroom atmosphere to work off their energies, it is here that the power of adult control is most required to protect pupils from their own exuberance. As a result, the courts have been rather strict in demanding an adequate degree of supervision.

There must be a teacher present on the playground. It is negligent for the teacher to be stationed in the building while the children are on the playground, even if the teacher is watching the pupils through a window. Further, if the teacher is absent from the play area, it is *no* excuse that the teacher is doing some other educationally valid task, such as holding a make-up class, collecting playground equipment, or supervising in another area. (Of course, the teacher will not be held personally liable where the principal has assigned him to be in two places at once, but he will be held liable if he undertakes too many duties on his own initiative.) The teacher must be present if the pupils pass by a dangerous situation to get to the play area, such as if they must cross a street.

Attendant to the necessity that there be supervision is the requirement that there be a *reasonable number* of qualified supervisors. It has been held to be a jury question as to whether a particular ratio of teachers to pupils is adequate supervision. Again, liability for the *assignment* of an inadequate number of teachers would fall upon the principal; however, it is clear that the teacher should have second thoughts before abandoning his post and asking another teacher already on duty to "cover" for him.

As with other problem areas, the question often arises as to whether inadequate supervision was the proximate cause of an injury—that is, whether the teacher should be held liable because of his absence where one pupil negligently or maliciously injures another. As discussed more fully in Chapter 2, the teacher will be held liable where the lack of supervision allows a dangerous situation to develop, and the injury results from the activities surrounding that dangerous situation. Thus, teachers have been held liable for injuries from roughhouse games such as "keep-away" and "blackout," and from dangerous situations such as pupils standing on swings, playing near driveways, and standing on fire escapes. Further, they have been made to pay for injuries resulting from malicious acts which are not instantaneous, such as fights, assaults, and rapes.

The theory for finding liability is that the teacher had he been present would have had time to observe the activity and to halt it before injury occurred. The teacher will not be held liable where the negligent or purposeful act of a pupil was very sudden and unexpected, under the theory that a supervising teacher could not have reacted in time to stop it. Thus teachers have been found not liable where two boys bumped heads while playing basketball, where a pupil fell due to a playful push, and where a pupil intentionally failed to avoid running into a passerby while running a footrace.

The case of *Dailey* v. *Los Angeles Unified School District* arose from an accident which occurred during a noon recess period. The school administration had assigned teachers to supervise the pupils who remained on the grounds for lunch, but, although the physical education department had responsibility for the gym area, on the day of the accident no one was supervising.

Two pupils left the lunchroom and went into the gym, where they proceeded to engage in "slap boxing," a playful type of openhanded boxing where the object is speed and skill. As they boxed for five or ten minutes, they attracted a crowd of onlookers. At one point one of the boxers fell backwards, hit his head, and died a short time afterwards. The pupil's estate sued the school for wrongful death, claiming that the negligent lack of proper supervision was a proximate cause of the pupil's death.

The trial court dismissed the suit, finding that, as a matter of law, even if a teacher were present he could not have halted the sudden fall.

However, the California Court of Appeals reversed the trial court and found for the pupil. The court noted evidence given during trial to the effect that as a general rule the teachers would halt slap boxing when they saw it. Therefore, the court reasoned, had a supervisor been present he would have acted to halt the slap boxing as soon as it started. That is, the court viewed the accident to be the foreseeable result of a build-up of rowdiness, rather than a sudden, unexpected fall.

It should be noted that the duty of supervision requires more than the mere presence of an adequate number of qualified personnel on the playground—the supervisors are required to take *affirmative steps* to protect the pupils under their care. Although the teacher does not have the duty of inspecting the playground equipment (that is the job of the Board of Education), the teacher does have a duty to warn the pupils about those dangerous conditions of which he is aware. Further, the teacher has an affirmative duty to *enforce* promulgated play rules, break up fights, and not lead children in dangerous games.

If the teacher is reasonably diligent in his general supervision and takes affirmative steps to correct unsafe situations, he cannot be said to be acting negligently; therefore, he will not be held liable for those unavoidable accidents which do occur. Once he has made the pupils aware of the play rules he need

not know what each pupil is doing during each minute of the recess period, nor must he halt normal playground games merely because there is an outside chance that something might happen. The courts require reasonable attention and common sense, not omniscience.

It should be noted that the above discussion concerning recess supervision duties also applies to those situations which have the same characteristics as formal recess periods: those times during the school day when pupils remain on the school grounds in an unstructured situation for significant periods of time. For example, courts have required supervision when pupils remain on the grounds for lunch, or gather in a communal area between exams.

Before and After School

The courts have not required supervision of pupils on school grounds before or after formal class hours, except when the situation takes on the characteristics of a recess, there is a dangerous condition present, or the school-sponsored activity is considered dangerous.

In general, supervision is not required during that time when pupils have arrived but classes have not yet begun; when they are leaving school for lunch off the school grounds or returning; or when they voluntarily remain after school to work on projects or to play on the playground. Since these situations are unlike recess periods in that the pupils are supposed to be engaged in purposeful activity and/or only a few pupils are involved, the courts have felt that the chances of accident are diminished to the point where it would be too burdensome to require a duty of supervision on the part of teachers.

The first exception to the general rule is that supervision must be supplied when a dangerous condition exists on the school grounds, since under such circumstances the chances of injury are greatly increased. For example, supervision has been required where trash was being burned on the grounds, and where icy conditions made snowballing particularly dangerous. (Thus far the mere existence of snow has not in itself been considered to be a dangerous condition requiring supervision, no doubt due to the heavy burden this would put upon school personnel.)

The second exception occurs when the situation takes on the characteristics of a recess, under the theory that the likelihood of accident increases when children are no longer "on the move" but must remain in a given area for any length of time. A school-sponsored carnival must be supervised. The most common requirement is that supervision is necessary when pupils wait for buses on the school grounds.

> In *Raymond v. Paradise Unified School District,* a seven-year-old pupil was hit by a school bus as he ran alongside of it in an attempt to be the first one on board. The bus stop was located at the high school and served pupils of all grades. No supervision was provided.
>
> At the conclusion of the presentation of evidence, the jury found the school district to be negligent and awarded damages to the pupil. The school district appealed, claiming that as a matter of law the court of appeals should find the pupil to be contributorily negligent and the school not negligent.
>
> The court of appeals affirmed the jury's decision. The court ruled that it was up to the jury to decide under the facts whether the pupil was contributorily negligent, and unless the jury's decision was clearly unreasonable the court of appeals would not disturb it. As to the negligence of the district, the court ruled that the jury was correct in finding there to be a proximate cause between the lack of supervision and the injury. The court noted that the school had no duty to provide bus transportation, but that once bus service was instituted, the district had a duty to do it safely. The opinion then went on to cite evidence that the bus stop was a busy area, with many students of all ages waiting for the frequently arriving buses. Under such circumstances, the failure to provide supervision created an unreasonable risk of injury and was the proximate cause of plaintiff's accident. The court stated that it was mindful of not placing extreme burdens upon the district, but that it was not overly difficult or impractical to place supervisors at the on-grounds bus stops.

In addition, after-school activities which may be considered dangerous must be supervised. Thus, there must be supervision of participants in wrestling matches, in the shop or laboratory, or at any other school-sponsored activities which involve more danger than the usual classroom activity.

Thus far the courts have refused to recognize the recess-like characteristics of those times before classes begin in the morning and after lunchtime when large numbers of pupils mill about on the school grounds, and have not required a duty of supervision. However, some judicial impatience with this rule has been registered, and so it is not clear whether the courts will continue to keep the burden of before- and after-school supervision off of school personnel.

Supervision is not required off school grounds for pupils traveling to and from school, although supervision is necessary for school-sponsored activities off school grounds.

Hallways

Generally speaking, the courts have recognized the substantial burden which would be placed upon teachers if they were made responsible for constant supervision of the school's hallways during the class day, and so they have refused to recognize any ongoing duty of supervision. However, once school personnel have noticed that the students are not using the break time to move from class to class but rather are using it more like a rowdy recess period, then, as reasonably prudent teachers, they must move to supervise the situation. A court will require something more than one or two previous isolated instances before it will rule that school personnel had notice of ongoing rowdyism in the hallways.

Under normal circumstances, there is no duty of supervision before the start of the classes or after school, nor is it necessary for the teacher to accompany pupils to the lavatory.

Of course, if the teacher happens to see a violation of the rules in the halls, he must take affirmative steps to remedy the situation; however, he need not intervene in seemingly harmless horseplay in the hallways.

First Aid

Although a teacher is not authorized to provide general medical treatment to a pupil, he has a duty to administer emergency aid. Thus, a very difficult situation for the teacher arises when a pupil has become injured. The teacher is required to take appropriate steps, but he may be held liable if he attempts to help too much as well as if he fails to do enough!

Although a citizen normally owes no duty to another citizen to summon a doctor or give first aid, the teacher-pupil relationship imposes certain protective duties upon the educator in the event of an "emergency." Whenever a teacher becomes aware of an injury to a pupil which requires immediate attention, the pupil's parents should be contacted so that they may consent to medical treatment of their child. If a parent cannot be reached and an emergency situation exists, the teacher is required to call a doctor to provide first aid. Where it is apparent that not one second can be wasted, the teacher has a duty to give first aid until the doctor arrives. (Once the doctor arrives the teacher must cease providing first aid.) For purposes of first aid, an "emergency" means a situation where *serious* injury is likely to ensue if *immediate* aid is not rendered —anything less than such a dire situation is not considered to be an "emergency." The exception is California, where by statute the teacher may apply "reasonable medical treatment" for any injury if the parent cannot be reached. If it is a true emergency, first aid may be administered even over the objections of the pupil.

In giving first aid, the teacher is not held to the standard of competence of a doctor or nurse, but he is required to act reasonably in applying his limited knowledge of medicine. Therefore, if the teacher engages in practices which a reasonable person should know are unwise or medically unsound, he may be found liable for a negligent application of his duty to provide first aid.

It was the second day of fall football practice, and the Louisiana sun poured down upon the sweating players. One of the players suddenly felt so woozy that he almost fainted on the playing field, and his teammates had to help him to the bus. After the team returned to the school, the pupil was placed on the gym floor and, after checking a first aid book, the coach applied first aid. Since the coach was convinced that the case merely involved mild heat exhaustion, he resisted suggestions by the parents of another student that a doctor be called—even as the pupil became ashen and lapsed into semiconsciousness. Finally a doctor was called, but by then the process had become irreversible and the student died.

After considering all the evidence, the court ruled that a reasonably prudent coach should have realized after a short time that an emergency existed and that the actions of the coach were improper under the circumstances. Then the court ruled that the negligent actions on the part of the coach were the proximate cause of the death of the student, since the coach's methods worked to deny the pupil qualified medical aid which might have saved him. Having found that the coach was negligent as well as that the negligence was the proximate cause of the pupil's death, the court then awarded damages to the estate of the pupil and to the pupil's parents. *Mogahgab* v. *Orleans Parish School Board.*

When the situation does not meet the criteria of an "emergency," it is assumed that the child's parents will deal with the problem; as a result, the teacher need not summon a doctor or provide first aid. In fact, as discussed in the section on *Medical Examination and Treatment,* in non-emergency situations the teacher has *no right* to give medical aid to a pupil (the pupil is incapable of giving consent), and may be held liable for so doing.

Non-Teachers

Many schools are supplementing their staff of certified teachers with uncertified personnel in the form of teacher's aides and student-teachers. Two questions arise:

1) May a teacher ever leave the supervision of pupils in the hands of uncertified personnel?

2) If uncertified personnel may undertake supervisory duties, what are the legal limits on their use?

Where there is no express statutory authority, it would seem that the school board may hire aides under its general authority to hire such assistants and employees as may be necessary. As an extension of this, it would seem to be permissible to leave a student-teacher in control of the classroom or playground— especially since such an action also serves the educational purpose of training a future teacher. Therefore, it would seem to not be negligence per se for the teacher to leave pupils under the supervision of uncertified personnel under normal circumstances, and the teacher will not be held liable for the sole reason that he has done so.

However, assuming the propriety of the use of uncertified personnel, nevertheless there are limitations. Firstly, the teacher must personally exercise control over those activities which carry with them high risks of injury; he cannot safely delegate the instruction or supervision of such activities to non-teachers. Although the cases have dealt only with student or student-teacher supervision of "dangerous" gym activities, the principle applies also to shop and laboratory activities, and to any other activities where there is more risk of injury than in the normal classroom situation.

Secondly, the person selected by the teacher must be qualified to handle the job. Persons who are not hired for their ability to deal with children, such as janitors, are not suitable choices. If the teacher is aware that the student-teacher or aide is incapable of handling the class in the teacher's absence, either because the student-teacher or aide lacks the ability to retain control over the class or because the class is particularly unruly, it will be negligence on the teacher's part to leave him alone with the pupils.

Summing up, it may be said that even in the absence of a statute the teacher will not be held liable for a pupil injury merely because the teacher has assigned an aide or student-teacher to supervise the pupils, unless the activity is one of high risk or unless the teacher should know that the person assigned is not able to retain control over the class.

A few states have cleared up the uncertainty by enacting statutes concerning the use of uncertified personnel. One form of the statute merely authorizes the use of uncertified personnel, so it would seem that the limitations discussed above would still apply: Cal. Educ. Code §§13561.1 (lunchroom supervisors), 13599 (aides), Conn. Gen. Stat. Ann. §10-235 (mentions student-teachers), 122 Ill. Stat. Ann. §34-18 (student-teachers, aides), Mass. Rev. Stat. §71-38 (aides), Minn. Stat. Ann. §123.35 (student-teachers). Nev. Rev. Stat. §391.100 (aides), N.Y. Laws 1969 Ch. 392 (aides), Ohio Rev. Code §3313. 643 (aides), Ore. Rev. Stat. §342.155 (student-teachers, aides), 24 Pa. Stat. Ann. 15.1519 (aides for driver training), 16 Vt. Stat. Ann. §203 (aides), Wash. Rev. Code Ann §28.76.-350 (student-teachers).

Another form of the statute not only authorizes the use of such personnel but specifies that they shall have the same authority as a certified teacher, and under such statutes there would be no restrictions upon their utilization: Kan. 1970 Sess. Laws, Ch. 278 (within limits set by state board), Ky. Rev. Stat. Ann. §161.180 (1970) (aides), N.C. Gen. Stat. §115-160.5 (student-teachers), N.D. Code §15-47-42 (student-teachers), 70 Okla. Stat. Ann. §1-18 (student-teachers), Tenn. Code Ann. §49-1301 (student-teachers), W. Va. Code §18A-5-1 (student-teachers, aides).

5

Supervision of the Class

Classroom Supervision

ASIDE from allowing dangerous situations to exist in the classroom, two types of situations arise in the classroom which may result in a lawsuit. The first occurs when the teacher absents himself from the room, and a pupil negligently or maliciously injures another pupil. The second involves a claim that the teacher failed to protect pupils from a known aggressive and violent pupil.

The teacher who has absented himself from the room is not automatically liable for every injury which occurs while he is gone. However, the courts have drawn a narrow line between liability and nonliability. As discussed more fully in Chapter 2, when the injurious act was sudden and unprovoked, the teacher will not be held liable, under the theory that the teacher could not have reacted fast enough to have stopped it; when the act came after a build-up of rowdyism, it becomes obvious that the teacher would have halted the disorder had he been present, and so the teacher will be held liable for any injury which results.

In *Christofides* v. *Hellenic Eastern Orthodox Christian Church of New York,* a pupil claimed that he was stabbed as a result of improper supervision.

Most students reported to class at 8:30 a.m. However, on this particular day the teacher was not there to preserve order. For the next twenty-five minutes the students ran around the room, engaging in fighting and horseplay. One pupil took out a knife, and for the next five to ten minutes he flashed it about. Finally he used it to stab plaintiff.

Defendant claimed that there should be no liability for the malicious act of a pupil unless the school personnel were aware of his vicious tendencies and failed to provide special protection. The court agreed that there must be some kind of warning; however, the court ruled in favor of plaintiff on the basis that, had the teacher been present as required, the build up of rowdiness would have served as enough warning. Further, the court noted the teacher's duty to disarm a pupil. Since the teacher would have taken the knife from the attacker right away, the pupil never would have been stabbed.

When the teacher is present, he owes a duty to his class to break up fights. However, he need not intervene in seemingly harmless horseplay.

The reasonably prudent teacher would take additional precautions to protect the class from a known violent or aggressive pupil. This is because while the teacher is not liable for sudden *unexpected* acts of pupils, where a pupil has known tendencies, quite simply, there is less that is unexpected. As in other areas of school law, the courts do not require the teacher to be omniscient or the insurer of his pupils' safety; rather, all they require is that, in light of the specific situation, the teacher act reasonably. To that end the teacher should ask himself: given the known tendencies of the pupil and the classroom circumstances (other demands upon the teacher's time and attention, seating possibilities, etc.), what steps would the reasonably prudent teacher take to keep the risk to the other students at a reasonable level? Where the teacher has taken reasonable precautions he will not be held liable for a sudden act which he could not have stopped.

As one aspect of the teacher's duties involving known violent or aggressive pupils, he must warn substitute teachers of such pupils' tendencies, so that each substitute will have adequate information upon which to base his decisions as to the degree of necessary supervision. If the teacher (or principal, where applicable) fails to advise the substitute teacher of special problems, he may be held liable for malicious injury caused by the aggressive pupil.

Shop and Laboratory

Shop and laboratory activities expose pupils to greater risks of injury than are present in the regular classroom. As a result, the reasonable teacher would not only supervise pupils' activities, he would be careful to provide the correct equipment and give detailed instructions as to the proper use of that equipment.

The most common occurrence is a pupil injury resulting from the lack of adequate instruction. Since the teacher must protect his pupils from their lack of maturity and judgment, "adequate instruction" not only includes the promulgation of safety rules *but also involves warnings which make clear the amount of danger inherent in the undertaking*. The courts have made it clear that any instruction which does not include information as to the *degree* of danger and the *gravity* of the injury which could result from not following the directions is legally inadequate. The shop teacher must detail the dangers of putting inappropriate objects into the machines, and when he becomes aware that a pupil is assembling a dangerous instrumentality (such as a cannon or rocket), he has a duty to carefully instruct the pupil as to the proper use of his creation. The laboratory instructor must fully explain experiment procedures; it is not acceptable to rely upon the text instruction, no matter how complete it is.

"It is not unreasonable to assume that it is the duty of the teacher of chemistry, in the exercise of ordinary care, to instruct students regarding the selection, mingling, and use of ingredients with which dangerous experiments are to be

accomplished, rather than to merely hand them a textbook
with general instructions to follow the text." *Mastrangelo v.
West Side Union High School District.*

Further, the instructor must set a good example; he must not
negate the effects of his instructions by violating safe procedures
while working within view of his pupils.

Since the courts are sensitive to pupils' complaints of inadequate instruction, it is very important for the teacher to be
certain that he has adequately instructed *each pupil.* A number
of cases in this area have turned out to be merely swearing
matches, with the instructor claiming that he gave adequate
instructions and the pupil claiming either that he did not receive
any instructions or that the instructions did not fully apprise
him of the danger involved. Thus, it is highly desirable that the
teacher keep a checklist of the date of each type of instruction,
the contents of the lecture, and a record of who was absent or
out of the room, so that the teacher may have *written* evidence
of the adequacy of his instruction. In addition, the teacher must
take pains to gauge the abilities of his pupils, and must make
absolutely certain that pupils with educational deficiencies (low
intelligence, poor understanding of English, hard of hearing,
etc.) understand the instructions.

There is a duty to provide a safe milieu for work. Although
the responsibility for providing suitable equipment rests with
the Board of Education, it is the responsibility of the teacher to
withhold any equipment which he should know has become
defective, to replace protective equipment which is broken or
missing, and to issue to the pupil that piece of equipment among
the several available which is suitable for the job at hand.
It is negligence for the teacher to place an unlabeled, uncorked bottle of acid on a shelf. Dangerous machines should
be locked when not in use. Further, storage areas should be
safe even though pupils are barred from them, since it is not
unforeseeable that pupils will be attracted to the many delights
within. (Although the teacher must keep the room safe, he is
not liable for injury caused when the pupils pilfer chemicals
either from the storage room or from open shelves and perform
unauthorized experiments in or out of class.) When pupils are

working with dangerous equipment or chemicals, it is negligence for the teacher to increase the danger by pitting them against each other in races.

There is a growing trend for states to enact a uniform statute which requires teachers and pupils to wear protective eye devices when working with hot, caustic, or explosive materials; when shaping, sawing, etc., metal; or when working on autos. Rather than free the teacher from responsibility, a statute of this sort implies liability in the event the teacher fails to adequately enforce it or sets a bad example by failing to follow it himself.

Where a teacher has violated any of the above rules and has negligently created a dangerous situation, he will not be insulated from liability merely because a pupil negligently acts upon the situation to injure another pupil. For example, one court ruled that a teacher who negligently failed to provide safety screens for a particular machine was liable for the injury to a pupil, even though that pupil was injured when a second pupil started the machine too soon.

Where a teacher has done all that a reasonable teacher would do to provide a generally safe working situation, he will not be liable for accidents.

The shop and lab teacher owe a duty of adequate supervision to the pupils, but, as with the normal classroom situation, the instructor will not be held liable where an injury occurring in his absence is the result of a sudden, unexpected act and is not the result of a build-up of rowdyism or a dangerous situation.

Of course, the teacher will be held liable if he himself errs during the lab or shop course. Teachers have been held liable when a demonstration experiment exploded and injured a pupil, and when a piece of equipment was dropped on a pupil's feet.

Physical Education

Since physical education activities provide more chances for injury than the normal school activities, the gym instructor owes added duties to his pupils. The courts have held that not only would the reasonable gym instructor provide supervision, but he would also prepare his pupils and the equipment properly so as to minimize chances for injury and take special precautions to prevent injury when directing the pupils in dangerous games. Of course, the gym instructor is not an insurer of the safety of his charges, and he will not be liable for injury where he has acted reasonably with regards to his duties.

As with other school personnel, the athletic instructor owes a duty of supervision and will be held liable for injuries resulting from roughhouse play or a dangerous situation in his absence. However, he will not be held liable for sudden acts which did not come as the result of a build-up of rowdiness, such as where a pupil runs into the flight of a thrown tennis ball or accidently kicks another pupil during exercises.

In addition to supervising activities, the athletic instructor has the duty to *prepare his pupils and the equipment properly* to help prevent injuries. This means that he must adequately instruct the students as to technique; further, he must take into account pupils' physical prowess and experience, and he may not assign exercises which are too advanced for their abilities or which may aggravate recent injuries that he knows about. The surrounding environment must be carefully controlled: mats should be properly placed, baseball bases must be secured to the gym floor when the game is played indoors, sharp projections are to be padded, overcrowding of the play area must be prevented, spectators should be kept out of the way of players, and pupils of *any* age must be supervised if they cross a street to get to the playing fields. If injury results from failure to do any of the above, the instructor will be open to liability.

Although the instructor must not allow pupils to use equipment which he should know is defective, he will not be held liable for equipment failure which could not be foreseen—as where stall bars suddenly come loose from the wall mounting.

Rightly or not, the courts have placed added duties upon teachers with regard to exercises which the *courts* feel are "dangerous." It is not easy to predict which exercises will be termed dangerous, since the courts often have little understanding of athletic instruction goals and techniques, but decisions are related to the court's assessment of the danger of injury from intended contact as well as unintended kicks, falls, pushes, etc. Thus, tag, tennis, handball, and touch football (when played by skilled participants) have been found to be not dangerous by various courts, while soccer, boxing, wrestling, and a dive and roll over two pupils have been found to be "dangerous." One court found headstands to be a dangerous activity, terming the exercise "absurd . . . dangerous . . . fantastic and perilous antics." Another court found that the use of apparatus to give physical fitness tests required added care, since the misuse of the equipment could result in a dangerous situation.

Once a court has determined that an athletic activity is dangerous, it will require instruction by a certified teacher—instruction by advanced students or student-teachers will not be acceptable, and the instructor will be held liable for allowing it in the event of an injury. Further, if the activity is competitive, the court will require that pupils be divided so that participants compete only against those of similar size (the match-up need not be exact)—a requirement that does not exist for "non-dangerous" games.

6

Responsibilities During School-Sponsored Activities

Safety Patrol

THE trend is toward legislative authorization of a safety patrol. Under the statutes in force in the following states, not only is the school permitted to form a safety patrol, but all persons involved in the supervision of the patrol are declared to be immune to liability: Alaska, California, Idaho, Illinois, Minnesota, Montana, Nevada, New Jersey, New York, Oregon, Utah, Washington, and Wisconsin.

The question arises as to the status of the safety patrol in those states where there is no enabling statutory authority, especially since there has been no higher court decision anywhere which has directly faced the issue. It would seem that the safety patrol is a logical and reasonable school activity in light of the well-settled power of the school to regulate pupils' activities while en route to and from school with regard to their safety. (See *What Conduct May Be Regulated.*) Therefore, based upon the general principles of school law, a safety patrol may be properly organized by a school even in those states which do not have safety patrol statutes.

Supervisors of safety patrols organized in such states will not enjoy immunity from liability, but on the other hand—as

48

we have seen in the discussion of other issues—neither is the teacher liable for all injuries which may occur. He is merely required to act reasonably in the discharge of his duties. For example, decisions in other areas of law indicate that it would be considered negligent to allow a pupil to act as a crossing guard if he has not been adequately instructed, or if he is physically unfit or emotionally unsuitable for the job, since the teacher should know that other children will be relying on him to protect their safety. However, where responsible pupils are selected for the patrol and are supervised in a reasonable manner, the supervising teacher will not be held liable solely because an accident occurs.

It should be made clear exactly what a "safety patrol" does. The purpose of a safety patrol seems to be limited to the controlling of *pupils* at crossings; with three statutory exceptions (California, Idaho, and Washington), pupils acting as a safety patrol are not deputized to halt or otherwise direct traffic.

Although a safety patrol is permissible, the school is never *required* to furnish traffic safety aid.

Field Trips

The teacher is held to no different standard of care on a field trip than in the classroom. He is required to act prudently in supervising the pupils' activities, warning them of dangers known to him and protecting them from their own immaturity. As in the classroom, he will not be held liable for injury due to sudden, unexpected acts. He is not required to inspect school vehicles used on the trip, but may assume that the Board of Education has supplied a suitable vehicle. In other words, the teacher is not an insurer of his pupils' safety and he will not be held liable for an injury if he has acted reasonably in the discharge of his duties.

It should be noted that the existence of a permission slip signed by a parent does *not* alter the teacher's duties. It merely serves to satisfy the teacher that the parent is informed of his child's whereabouts, and does not serve as a consent to negligence. Some permission notes contain a promise on the part of the parents that they will not sue in the event of an injury to their child. However, such notes have limited significance since it is the child who sues for the major portion of damages in the event of injury, and it is legally impossible for a parent to sign away his child's legal rights.

Although the standard of care—that of a reasonable teacher —is the same on a field trip as in the classroom, what it takes to fulfill that standard may be different in the field trip situation. Where the pupils are excited about the trip and/or are visiting a site containing dangerous machinery or natural wonders, the reasonably prudent teacher would recognize the increased chance of injury and would provide more vigilant supervision than he might during the normal class day. Just how diligent the teacher must be—how many additional supervisory personnel must accompany the class, how closely the class must be watched, which sites are too dangerous to visit at all, etc.— has not yet been outlined by the courts. Thus the teacher's only guide is his own answer to that question which he should constantly be asking himself, that question which a judge or jury will be asking if an accident occurs: what would a reasonably prudent teacher under similar circumstances do or not do in order to avoid an unreasonable risk of injury to the pupils in his class? Asking the question is 99% of the battle, since the teacher's consciously exercised judgment will no doubt be correct; it is only when the teacher fails to consider the ramifications of his actions that he places himself in real danger of a lawsuit.

Interscholastic Athletics

School-sponsored athletics are a widely accepted part of the educational process, and so the coach is vested with the same authority in the control of his team that a teacher has over his class. Of course, along with the rights of a teacher come responsibilities equivalent to those of the physical education instructor, discussed in the section on *Physical Education.*

School personnel owe a duty of crowd control during sporting events, and spectators must be kept out of the way of players. However, where teachers have been assigned to crowd control and reasonable efforts are made to prohibit spectators from entering the playing area, instructors will not be liable for injury resulting from a spectator's entering a restricted area nor for an accident to a spectator who is so unfamiliar with the sport as to foolishly wander into an obviously dangerous area.

The coach taking his players to an "away game" is not an insurer of their safety and will not be held liable for any injury. He need only act reasonably with regards to their safety. For example, the coach may assume that the Board of Education has supplied him with a suitable vehicle, and he need not inspect it for defects.

The athletic association, school, or coach may make rules for school athletes which are reasonable, nondiscriminatory, and related to the educational purposes of interscholastic athletics. See Chapter Seven, page 57, for a more complete discussion of the school's authority over extracurricular activities in general and athletics in particular, and pages 64–65 for an analysis of recent decisions involving hair regulations.

School-Sponsored Events

Although normally it is considered to be too burdensome to place a duty of supervision upon school personnel outside of school hours, when the school has sponsored an event it must accept the duty to provide adequate supervision. In a legal sense the school carnival or dance becomes a "recess," and, as such, must be supervised so as to prevent injuries due to a build-up of rowdyism.

In *Lehmuth* v. *Longbeach Union High School District,* a spectator to a homecoming parade was injured when the hitch to one of the floats came loose and the float struck him. Since the accident occurred in California, he sued the school as well as the supervisors on the basis of inadequate supervision. After considering the evidence the jury found in favor of the injured spectator, and the defendants appealed.

On appeal, the Supreme Court of California affirmed the jury's decision. The court ruled that the school has a duty to supervise school-sponsored events both on and off school property in order to protect the public from youthful impetuosity. Since the school has such a duty by law, it was permissible for the jury to find that the facts disclosed negligence in the failure to supervise the float connection.

Counseling

Only one case concerning the legal duties involved in counseling has reached a higher court. In *Bogust* v. *Iverson,* the parents of a college student claimed that the counselor was negligent in not notifying them of their child's depressed state, not securing psychological services for the student, and terminating the counseling relationship where the student later committed suicide. In finding for the counselor, the court recognized that he was held merely to the standard of a reasonable educator, not a psychiatrist. The opinion noted that, since the pupil had psychological problems previous to the counseling, it was mere speculation that the termination of the counseling resulted in the suicide. Although this decision leaves many questions unanswered, its importance lies in its acceptance of general negligence rules in counseling situations. That is, the counselor is not required to be omniscient, nor he is an insurer of the pupil's safety; rather, he is merely expected to act reasonably under the circumstances.

Even where a counseling session involves possible disciplinary action, a pupil has no right to insist upon his attorney being present.

III

The Teacher's Rights

7

The Enforcement of
School Rules

THE right to attend public schools is conditional upon the
pupil's acceptance of reasonable school rules. The school personnel stand in place of the parents (*in loco parentis*) in school
related matters, and so they may punish pupils who violate
those rules.

Just as parents may be brought to account for abusing their
parental rights to discipline their children, the rights of school
authorities to punish pupils have legal boundaries. If the teacher
remains within these limits in maintaining control of the
classroom, he will be legally protected; however, if he oversteps
his *in loco parentis* powers, he will open himself to liability.
The boundaries set by the courts and legislature involve:

1) which in-school acts may be punished;
2) which off-grounds acts may be punished; and
3) the extent to which violative conduct may be punished.

What Conduct May Be Regulated

School personnel may punish pupils for any in-school acts
which are considered to impair the educational environment

57

and/or undermine the teacher's authority, and a rather broad view of their powers is taken. Thus it has been held that teachers may punish pupils who are tardy or truant, smoke on school grounds, cheat on examinations, disrupt others, fail to hand in homework or hand in someone else's work, come to class unprepared, fight in the halls, act insolently, use profanity, insult or strike the teacher, or engage in malicious destruction of property. Pupils may be required to follow reasonable classroom procedures, stay out of the teacher's chair or private papers, cease wearing destructive and noisy metal heel plates, wear proper attire at graduation ceremonies, name others who are breaking the rules, and remain on the school grounds during the entire school day—including lunch time. (The exception is Hawaii, where by statute the principal must honor a parent's written request to allow his child to leave during class breaks.) Those not enrolled in a particular school may be barred from visiting it during school hours. A pupil receiving insufficient grades may be denied graduation. School personnel may promulgate driving regulations which limit pupils' operation and parking of autos on school property or surrounding streets during school hours, and may even prohibit pupils from driving to school altogether.

The above reasonable rules may be enforced even over the objections of parents; in fact, the *pupil* may be punished where his *parent* has ordered him to disobey a school rule. School personnel may bar married students from taking part in non-academic activities. (However, a pupil may not be suspended or expelled merely for being married.) The teacher's authority is not only over pupils in his own room, but also extends to all pupils attending the school. School regulations need not list every manner of offense; the rules need only be sufficiently precise so that the standards are understood by the student body. The rules need not be officially adopted by the Board of Education to be enforceable; where the board has remained silent the teacher may make reasonable rules on his own initiative, and some rules of conduct are so basic that it is assumed that pupils know to obey them even if the teacher has not mentioned them.

Not only may teachers make rules concerning classroom con-

duct, but they may also issue directives concerning pupil activity while traveling to and from school. Such power is inherent in the school's function, and in addition has been recognized by the legislature in many states. For example, the school may require that pupils go straight home after school or refrain from fighting while en route, and may punish them for violation of the rules. (Although school personnel have the *power* to regulate pupil conduct en route if they so wish, they do not have the *duty* to provide supervision.)

Over and above the right to control students while en route to and from school, teachers may regulate other out-of-school activity which *directly* affects the successful operation of the educational process—the criterion is whether the conduct is significantly deleterious to the authority of school personnel or the morale of the pupils, not the time and place of the conduct.

> "[T]he school authorities have the power to [punish] a pupil for an offense committed outside of school hours, and not in the presence of the teacher, which has a direct and immediate tendency to influence the conduct of other pupils while in the schoolroom, to set at naught the proper discipline of the school, to impair the authority of the teachers, and to bring them into ridicule and contempt. Such power is essential to the preservation of order, decency, decorum, and good government in the public schools." *State ex rel. Dresser v. District Board.*

The courts have upheld punishment meted out for nighttime destruction of school property, calling the teacher derogatory names in the presence of other students, defying disciplinary procedures in public, and for continually abusing smaller children passing by shortly after arriving home from school. In one case the court approved the suspension of a pupil who had knifed a neighbor until such time as the school could determine whether the presence of the pupil at school would endanger the safety of the other pupils and school personnel. Although earlier cases upheld the school's right to punish pupils for immoral conduct occurring outside of school, the times have changed and it is doubtful whether the school could so punish a pupil unless it could show strong effects upon the health or morale of the student body. To illustrate how views have changed, in a 1924 case a court upheld the punishment of a *college* coed for smoking in public, riding about town in a convertible on a man's lap, and other miscellaneous "acts of indiscretion."

School authorities may regulate the activities of school-connected organizations, or may ban them completely, in order to promote the pupils' safety, encourage the concentration upon academics, or protect against bad influences. For example, the chance to play interscholastic athletics is considered to be a privilege, not a right, and the coach, school board, or the athletic association may place reasonable, nondiscriminatory restrictions upon participation (even if such action destroys a pupil's chances of earning a college scholarship). Athletes may be held to stricter standards of conduct than the remainder of the school body as a condition of their remaining on the school team or retaining their "letters." Married students may be barred from taking part in extracurricular activities. Another example involves the public school fraternity, sorority, or secret society, i.e., a group of pupils that chooses its members instead of accepting anyone who wishes to join. The school board has inherent power to regulate or ban such groups, based upon its right to control disruptive influences. In addition, a great many states have embodied the antipathy toward secret clubs in statute, either banning sororities, fraternities and secret societies from every school in the state or expressly recognizing the power of the local school districts to regulate or prohibit them if they wish. The school's inherent power to suspend or expel pupils who continue to violate such rules is supplemented by statutory authority in most states.

The courts have been so solicitous of the teacher's preeminent position in the classroom that they have even allowed the punishment of pupils for conduct of the parents which has tended to undermine the teacher's authority.

"The right of a child to attend a public school is dependent upon the good conduct of the parent as well as the child. Both must submit to the reasonable rules and regulations of the school, and the parent must so conduct himself as

not to destroy the influence and authority of the school management over the children whenever he comes into contact with the school authorities, whether commissioners, officers, or teachers, under circumstances where his conduct would be likely to influence the conduct of his children."
Board of Education v. Purse.

It has been ruled permissible to punish a child when his parent refuses to abide by a reasonable school rule, continually allows his child to be tardy and absent, or insults the teacher in front of the class. Several states have made it a criminal misdemeanor to upbraid, insult or abuse a teacher in front of a pupil or to disrupt the school.

The school may make reasonable regulations involving the access to pupils by outside persons. For example, the school may require that a police officer who has come onto the premises to question students speaks to them only in the presence of school personnel. However, school policies must give way to a valid warrant for a student's arrest.

Normally, the courts will presume the correctness and reasonableness of school rules and discipline, and it will be up to the pupil suing to show an abuse of discretion.

School authorities have the responsibility for assigning children to grade level, and they may take into account each child's ability, knowledge and training as well as age. Pupils may be classified within grade level by learning ability and may be assigned to classrooms or groupings within classrooms on that basis. Such decisions by school personnel take precedence over parental desires, and will be upheld by the courts unless the assignments are arbitrary or motivated by racial discrimination.

Absent statute, the parent is not responsible for damage done by his child. However, the child himself may be required to pay for malicious damage to school property, and many states have recognized the parental responsibility by enacting statutes which require the parents to pay for malicious damage to school property done by their children.

Limitations Upon the Teacher's Authority

In spite of the above-mentioned broad powers, the teacher's jurisdiction does have limits. Firstly, the teacher has no *in loco parentis* control over children who are not presently attending his school. There is legal authority that school regulations are without effect during summer vacation. If a pupil has earned his diploma, it may not be withheld from him, nor may he be disciplined for an act which occurs *after* he has completed his academic work for graduation. School personnel may not require that a pupil complete his punishment in another school district as a requirement for transfer to the new system, nor may the teacher in the new district punish him for that prior act.

Secondly, the teacher has no power to intrude into the pupil's home life: "In the home, parental authority is and should be supreme, and it is misguided zeal that attempts to wrest it from them." *Hobbs v. Germany.* For example, teachers may not demand that pupils remain at home and do homework at specific times each night, ban attendance at private parties, nor require a pupil to take part in a school activity which violates the religious or moral teachings of his home. Although the legislature may require the taking of certain courses by statute, since the choice of school subjects is so determinative of a child's future it is presumed that parents have more knowledge of the best long-term interests of the child than do local school authorities; therefore, the parents may successfully prohibit their child from taking any course or subject not made compulsory by the state legislature. (However, a parent may not disrupt the educational process by insisting that his child be allowed to take a course or use a book not offered at the school, use methods of study which interfere with others, or be placed in a class where his presence will retard the advancement of others in the class.)

Thirdly, it is outside the teacher's *in loco parentis* powers to enforce rules which are not designed to achieve educational goals. Thus, it has been ruled that the teacher may not require pupils to perform manual labor on a regular basis, where the requirement was made not for disciplinary or educational purposes but merely as a method of achieving upkeep of the school. Teachers are not judicial officers and so have no authority to fine pupils for wrongful acts. Neither may they demand fees from the pupils for their services. The school cannot prevent pupils from buying food and school supplies from other than the school store, where the sole purpose is to create an economic monopoly. Although extracurricular activities may be regulated so as to encourage safety or scholarship, absent specific statutory authorization (only New Jersey has such a statute), a limitation on the activities of a school band for the purpose of protecting professional musicians from competition is void. Since it serves no educational purpose, a school may not punish a pupil who is too poor to pay for intentional damage to property, nor make attendance at graduation ceremonies a requirement of graduation. Pupils may not be punished for accidental or careless damage to property, nor for acts of other pupils, nor be denied an education merely for being married. A pupil may not be excluded from class solely because she is an unwed mother; it must be shown that she is so lacking in moral character as to taint the education of the other students.

The changing grooming patterns of students have elicited much comment in many communities, and have greatly strained those courts which have attempted to find an answer to this thorny issue. Many students now feel that the school has no right to regulate their attire or hair style, since such regulation of their personality is akin to an invasion of privacy and is not subject to the authority of educators. On the other hand, many parents and educators feel that it is their responsibility to guide the grooming of pupils, and that the removal of grooming rules will encourage the more bizarre-looking students to turn school into a circus. One battleground has been the court system—during the period from January 1969 to April 1971 there were more than forty cases decided in state courts of appeals and supreme courts, and federal district courts and courts of appeals, which is a prodigious number of cases to be decided in such a period of time on such a narrow issue.

However, the spate of decisions has confused the issue rather than clarified it. All the courts have agreed upon the basic principles:

1) Educators in public schools have powers to regulate only those pupil activities which adversely affect the educational process or the health and safety of the students;

2) A pupil's constitutional rights may be limited only when the exercise of those rights substantially interferes with the educational process;

but they are all over the field in applying the general principles to specific cases. Some courts have ruled that grooming is expressive to the point where it enjoys First Amendment "freedom of speech" protection—a substantial constitutional protection which puts a heavy burden of proof on the school limiting it. Other courts have ruled that grooming is an element of privacy which enjoys Fourteenth Amendment protection such that it may not be limited except by "due process," that is, by rules which are fair, nondiscriminatory, and reasonably related to educational goals. Some courts have merely looked to the fairness of the rule and have ducked the constitutional issues, while one federal court refused to rule at all and opined that it was up to the state legislature to make uniform rules for all schools in the state. A few courts have ruled that a pupil may sue under 42 U.S.C.A. § 1983, a federal statute which is designed to protect "civil rights."

Mainly, the courts vary widely in the quality of proof they will accept in order to uphold the school's regulation. Some courts have placed a heavy burden upon the principal and have required such things as proof of actual, substantial disruptions or safety or health hazards caused by grooming, a written code which is explicit on what constitutes violation and is not based upon unreasonable classifications, and statistical data to support the school's claims. Such courts refuse to acknowledge that the school can base regulations upon aesthetics or the desire for conformity, that requiring pupils to follow rules regardless of content promotes respect for authority, or that pupils can be required to moderate their appearance because of over-reaction and physical attacks upon them by other pupils. If the school complains of health or safety problems, the court is likely to inquire why teachers or female students are not similarly regulated as to hair length, and why narrower rules directed specifically to the health or safety problem are not promulgated.

On the other hand, other courts have relied upon the professional expertise of educators and have based their decisions upon such minimal evidence as the principal's opinions that: unrestricted grooming *might* be a diverting influence on the student body; long hair would injure the school's "image"; a change in hair style *causes* a pupil's grades to go down; or, school personnel are responsible for regulating the aesthetics of the student population. Certain courts have been so anxious to uphold the authority of school personnel that they have based their decisions upon such nonsense as preventing "unrestrained anarchy," preventing hurt feelings on the part of these students who cannot grow facial hair, providing a method of telling the boys from the girls, and blaming long-haired students for being picked upon!

Regulation of hair length with regard to extracurricular activities is also being attacked in the courts, and the decisions in this area are no more uniform. In a California Federal District Court case, the court upheld regulation of hair length based upon opinion testimony that long hair hurts performance and that obedience to rules aids discipline and morale on the team, and an Arkansas Federal District Court allowed regulation of hair style in a school band. On the other hand, a Vermont District Court voided hair regulations for athletes, saying that it is illegal to allow one class of students to participate in extracurricular athletics while withholding the privilege from another class of students unless the differentiation is necessary to serve compelling school interests. The court found eligibility based upon hair length to be not justifiable as a mere enforcement of the coach's personal tastes, noting the lack of hard and fast evidence that long hair *per se* causes disruption and/or poor performance. As to the argument that obedience to rules builds character, the court said:

> "The coach's right to regulate the lives of his team members does have limits though. A coach may not demand obedience to a rule which does not in some way further other proper objectives of participation and performance. It is

bootstrap reasoning indeed to say that disobedience of any rule weakens the coach's authority or shows a lack of desire on the part of the competitor thus justifying obedience to any rule however arbitrary." *Dunham v. Pulsifer.*

What does the foregoing discussion mean to the public school teacher? Perhaps the best summary of the situation was made in *Jeffers* v. *Yuba City Unified School District:*

"The legal reasoning of these opinions is in complete disarray and both the nature and extent of the right of the male student to wear his hair at any desired length are far from being settled issues."

Further, it does not appear that the issue will be soon clarified since the only body which could set standards which would affect every judicial district, the United States Supreme Court, has shown no interest whatsoever in accepting grooming cases as of the time this book goes to press. Due to the uncertainty of the law and the likelihood of suits by pupils affected by grooming rules, it is strongly recommended that decisions concerning dress regulations be made at the school board level and only after extensive consultation with students, parents, educators, and the board's lawyer. Under no circumstances should a teacher attempt to make and enforce his own dress rules for his classroom.

Last—but not least—pupils do not forfeit their constitutional rights to "freedom of speech" by attending school. Our courts have always been zealous in protecting the freedom of speech of adults, and recent cases have expressly decided that such protection extends to pupils' distribution of "underground" newspapers and political literature on school grounds.

"Clearly then, freedom of speech, which includes publication and distribution of newspapers, may be exercised to its fullest potential *on school grounds* so long as it does not unnecessarily interfere with normal school activities. Administration can properly regulate the times and places within the school building at which newspapers may be distributed. Obviously the First Amendment does not require that students be allowed to read newspapers during class periods. Nor should loud speeches or discussion be tolerated in the halls during class time. A proper regulation as to "place" might reasonably prohibit all discussion in the school library. Administration may not, however, apply regulations as to "time" or "manner" in a discriminatory fashion." *Sullivan v. Houston Independent School District.*

Such decisions are based upon the premise that "education" is more than mere supervised and ordained classroom discussion, but rather is defined broadly to include communication amongst students through both formal and informal channels. As such, in-school communication may not be regulated merely because school personnel or political figures are held up to ridicule, or because students with opposing views may wrongfully overreact to the publication.

For purposes of constitutional law, "speech" includes not only spoken and written *words,* but also *any other activity which is designed to communicate a point of view on an issue.* For example, it has been held to be a protective activity to wear a button or armband on school grounds, take part in a nonviolent, nondisruptive demonstration, refuse to stand during the singing of the National Anthem, or refuse to take part in or leave the room during the Pledge of Allegiance, where such activity is designed to communicate a political viewpoint. Where the activity is protected, the student may not be punished or be forced to segregate himself from his fellow pupils.

No municipal authority has the right to prohibit the distribution of literature in public areas such as parks or public sidewalks.

Although students may not be *silenced,* the time and manner of their activities on school grounds may be *limited* when their conduct tends to "materially and substantially interfere with the requirements of appropriate discipline in the operation of the school," under the school's preeminent right to provide a suitable educational process.

"But conduct by the student, in class or out of it, which for any reason—whether it stems from time, place, or type of behavior—materially disrupts classwork or involves substantial disorder or invasion of the rights of others is, of course, not immunized by the constitutional guarantee of freedom of speech." *Tinker v. Des Moines Independent Community School District.*

Therefore, pupils may be disciplined for interfering with the operation of the school by engaging in a boycott of school facilities or a "sit-in," disrupting a sporting event, or engaging in violent protest. Although the mere wearing of buttons is a protected activity, when the passing out of the buttons involves an "unusual degree of commotion, boisterous conduct, a collision with the rights of others, an undermining of authority, and a lack of order, discipline, and decorum," the buttons may be banned. Even though students may adopt an object of clothing as a symbol of unity, when that symbol becomes the excuse for disruption and the bullying of other pupils, then its wearing may be prohibited. Speech which has incited students to do acts which materially intrude upon school work is not protected. Greater restrictions may be placed upon the use of public school grounds than are permissible on college campuses. Although a pupil may not be punished solely for attending a demonstration, he may be punished—even suspended—for regular and repeated absences from school caused by the protest activities. Again it should be noted that pupils engaging in "free speech" activity may be punished only when the communication has resulted in *substantial and material* interference with the functioning of the school; that is, to be outside the area of First Amendment protection there must occur something more than the mere mild curiosity or temporary distraction from school work which is to be expected when unpopular or controversial opinions are expressed.

School personnel do not have to wait until trouble actually begins before acting. Pupil conduct may also be limited if it has not yet caused disruption but there is a clear and present danger that material interference with school operations will come about. However, it should be noted that when school personnel act in such a situation—when disruption actually has not yet occurred—there is a heavy burden upon them to justify their limitation of constitutional rights. There must be a reasonable fear of *substantial* disruption. The danger must be immediate. There must be no other practical alternatives. A pupil's *intent* to cause disruption is not enough to merit regulation by the school; it must appear to the objective bystander that he is succeeding. It is not enough that a pupil's speech or acts merely add in a general way to student unrest or that school authorities have an unspecific fear that "something" might happen.

For example, the mere distribution of an underground newspaper or political literature which states unpopular opinions is not considered to be an immediate threat to the school, and so is a protected activity. Requiring pupils to submit an underground newspaper or political literature for approval before distribution is unconstitutional censorship, although the school may require prior approval of material to be passed out on the grounds by nonstudents. However, where literature strongly urges immediate physical actions and threatens to precipitate substantial disorder, it may be suppressed.

Although the wearing of buttons or armbands normally is not considered to cause a clear and present danger to the educational process, where the specific situation is such that fear of immediate substantial disruption is *well-founded* and *specific,* the wearing of such insignia may be banned in advance of disorder. Such a case was *Guzick* v. *Drebus,* where the court found evidence of extreme racial tensions at a high school, with some students just waiting for an excuse to do battle.

Finally, it is a reasonable rule that there is to be no soliciting of funds for any cause on the school grounds, even if no past disruption has been shown, since the school has a right to protect students from the social pressure of multiple solicitations.

Recently the courts have had to deal with the conflict between the various statutes making the disturbing of schools a misdemeanor and the First Amendment protection of protest activities. Of course, there is no First Amendment issue when the disruption is accomplished by the garden variety troublemaker; however, when the disturbance is caused by those who are attempting to petition for a change in policies or to protest some occurrence, then the societal value protecting free speech is on a collision course with the value we place upon the educational process. The courts are now in the process of drawing that fine line which separates the legitimate protection of the school environment from unconstitutionally overbroad statutory language which unnecessarily impinges on free speech. For example, a city ordinance which bans *all* picketing within 150 feet of a school is unconstitutional and void, since it does not separate disruptive activities from peaceful, quiet expressions of opinion. Although a California Court of Appeals has found the California statute barring disruption of schools to be unconstitutionally overbroad, courts in several other states have upheld similar statutes and it is this view which seems more correct.

It should be noted that obscenity is not considered to be speech which is protected by the Constitution, and as such it may be barred from the school grounds. Further, obscenity restrictions for juveniles may be more rigorous than would be allowed for adults.

However, it is not adequate merely to designate certain words as offensive or "obscene." Obscenity is more than a list of "dirty words," it is a feeling of offensiveness which is gained by reading or hearing the words in context. Thus words which might normally be considered vulgar in everyday use may be properly included in serious academic discussion. For example, in *Keefe* v. *Geanakos* the court allowed classroom discussion of a scholarly article which analyzed the use of offensive language by youths to irritate their elders. Further, the courts will require consistency in the school's treatment of obscenity. In several cases the courts refused to allow pupils to be punished for possessing or discussing literature on school grounds which contained offensive words, where such words were included in books or magazines that were to be found in the school library. In one case the court refused to allow a college newspaper to be banned from campus as obscene where other publications sold on campus contained similar words.

Search of Desk or Locker

The Fourth Amendment to the United States Constitution provides that a person's possessions shall be free from "unreasonable" searches and seizures. Countless court decisions have wrestled with problems surrounding the issuance of search warrants, warrantless searches, search of vehicles, etc. However, the complicated issues surrounding these provisions do not apply to teachers, school officers, or other private citizens, since these particular constitutional provisions are only intended to regulate the conduct of law enforcement officials.

Nevertheless, two questions arise. Firstly, when may a private citizen engage in a search of another person's possessions? Secondly, are the rules different when that private citizen happens to be a teacher or principal who wishes to search the desk or locker of a pupil under his control?

The average citizen has no right to engage in the search of another person's possessions or to authorize the police to do so. This is not based upon the constitutional requirements surrounding search, but rather upon such notions as privacy and trespassing. Thus a landlord cannot cause a tenant's premises to be searched, nor may a hotel open a guest's room for inspection. Even if a person has access to another's property for limited purposes, this does not free him to give permission for the police to search it. For example: an employer who has access to an employee's desk for business purposes still does not have sufficient dominion over the desk to authorize police search; although hotel personnel may enter rooms to clean them, they may not open them for police search; and, although a coin locker company may have an implied right to inspect the lockers in order to determine abandoned items, there is no right for them to consent to a police search of any rented locker. Even where a person has sufficient control over an area to authorize a search by police, he still may not consent to a search of locked containers resting there which are owned by someone else. (A person finding an object may make a casual inspection so as to identify ownership, and may call police if he discovers something illegal.)

A parent may authorize police to search those rooms in his home in which his child lives as well as consent to a police search of his child's belongings, as part of a parent's almost unlimited right to control his child.

As has been noted many times in this book, the teacher's

relation to his pupils is such that additional rights and duties exist over and above those amongst the general public but less than those existing with parents. As a result, the courts have ruled that teachers have greater rights to engage in the search of a pupil's property and to authorize police search than if they were average citizens *as long as an educational goal is being served*. This means that a teacher or principal has the right to inspect a pupil's desk or locker—and the property therein— under the school's preeminent right to maintain an atmosphere conducive to education and to protect the pupils from being enticed into illegal activities. It is of no matter that a pupil is given "exclusive" use of a desk or locker; this exclusivity is in relation to other students and the general public, and the use is non-exclusive in relation to the school.

> "Indeed, it is doubtful if a school would be properly discharging its duty of supervision over the students if it failed to retain control over the lockers. Not only have the school authorities the right to inspect, but this right becomes a duty when suspicion arises that something of an illegal nature may be secreted there." *People v. Overton.*

However, the school does not possess the right to engage in blanket searches of pupils' facilities where there is no *specific* cause for fear, since merely looking for "something" would not achieve educational goals, nor is a search for private purposes allowed. It has been held that a search by school personnel may be undertaken only when they have a "reasonable belief" that the student is utilizing the facilities for a use which is illegal or interferes with discipline. In order to call in the police, the teacher must either have found the contraband, or must have knowledge which leads him to believe that there is *probably* an illegal use. Note that there is a higher standard for requesting a police search than for doing it oneself ("probable cause" vs. "reasonable belief"), since police are government officials and come under the strict requirements of the U.S. Constitution, as discussed above.

(The above rules apply to school-initiated search. When a police officer comes to the school with a search warrant to search a portion of the premises, the matter is entirely out of the school's hands and the teacher or principal has no choice but to allow the search.)

If an illegal object is found in the search, the teacher may confiscate it since the pupil can have no rights of ownership over an illegal item. However, if the teacher comes into possession of items that merely disrupt the educational process (squirt guns, etc.), it is the limit of the teacher's authority to require that it be removed from the school situation. This is because the pupil remains the owner of the object, and the teacher's powers are limited to the educational milieu.

Suspension and Expulsion

The teacher has authority to utilize a variety of punishments to maintain order and discipline, up to and including suspension. For minor offenses, the pupil may be temporarily removed from the classroom (physical force may be used if the pupil refuses to leave), detained after school, or limited in his non-academic school activities. For serious infractions, the pupil's credits and/or diploma may be withheld. As part of the teacher's inherent right to maintain order in the classroom, the courts have ruled that the teacher has the common law right to suspend a pupil who threatens the stability of the classroom and to set reasonable conditions for his return.

However, as schools have moved from one-room institutions where the teacher was also usually the "principal teacher" to organizations with many layers of administration, most state legislatures have added a heavy overlay of statutory law to the common law principles and most local school boards have promulgated additional provisions. As a result, the teacher would be well advised to consult with his principal concerning the exact statutory language in his state and the procedures which have been established in his school district before attempting to banish any pupil from the classroom for any significant length of time.

The teacher should be aware that all statutes must be *interpreted* by courts, and judges are extremely sensitive to two considerations when considering suspension or expulsion cases:

1) the seriousness of denying a pupil access to education, even for a short time; and
2) the purpose of suspension or expulsion as being more the protection of classroom stability than the improvement of the pupil.

Therefore, the school must be ready to show to a court not only that the pupil violated the express terms of a rule, but also that the continued presence of the pupil would have a demoralizing effect upon the pupils and/or a deteriorating effect upon discipline.

Courts have held that suspension or expulsion must be based upon misconduct which is gross or persistent. A pupil may not be kept from pursuing his education for a "petty or trivial offense," or because his personality or activities are distasteful to the authorities. Marriage or bearing an illegitmate child is not in itself sufficient grounds for expulsion. A pupil may not be suspended solely because he failed courses. Although a pupil may be suspended for malicious destruction of property, he may not be punished for mere carelessness. A pupil may not be suspended for failure to pay for vandalism damage where such nonpayment is not willful but is the result of his family's inability to raise the money.

Where the statute or local school board rules expressly state which school official has the power to suspend or expel students, these powers may not be delegated to lesser personnel and only that official may exercise them. If there are no statutory or school board guidelines, suspension can last the length of the school year but no longer.

An issue which is presently being tested in the courts is whether a pupil has a constitutional "due process" right to a hearing prior to being suspended or expelled. Some courts have looked to the traditional *in loco parentis* powers of the schools in ruling that no hearing is necessary, while other courts have followed the lead of recent cases involving suspension from college in extending a right to some type of hearing (i.e., the right to be informed of the charges and to offer evidence on one's behalf). One recent New York decision extended the right to a hearing to any serious punishment, and required the school to provide a hearing where the pupil's right to take the New York Regents Examination was revoked due to cheating.

Even those courts which require due process hearings for suspension do not require extensive formalities for lesser punishments, but the trend is to require some procedure which allows the student to be heard. In a very recent case, a pupil complained that his athletic "letter" was summarily taken away from him for an infraction of the school's code for athletes. The court ruled that, although no formal hearing was necessary or desirable, the student must be provided some informal right to discuss the issues and defend his actions prior to the imposition of punishment.

Use of Corporal Punishment to Enforce Rules

New Jersey is the only state which does not recognize the right of the school teacher to utilize physical punishment as a means of enforcing school rules. Many states have acknowledged the right to use corporal punishment by court decision, while others have enacted statutory authorization. The few states which have not faced the issue could be expected to go along with the traditional outlook when faced with a test case.

Since corporal punishment involves the use of physical force upon the person of a pupil, the legal rules surrounding its use are discussed in Chapter 8 in relation to assault and battery problems.

8

Assault and Battery Problems

The Law of Assault and Battery

GENERALLY, persons in our society are protected from being touched in an offensive manner or being threatened with such unwanted contact. As discussed previously, where such unwanted contact occurs unintentionally, an action for negligence may result. However, where a person *intends* to make a contact which he should know would be offensive to the person touched, he may be held liable for assault and battery.

> "An assault may be defined as any intentional, unlawful offer of corporal injury to another by force, or force unlawfully directed toward the person of another, under such circumstances as create a well-founded fear of imminent peril, coupled with the apparent ability to effectuate the attempt if not prevented.
> A battery, or assault and battery, is the willful touching of the person of another by the aggressor or by some substance put in motion by him; or, as it is sometimes expressed, a battery is the consummation of the assault." *Tinkler v. Richter.*

Certain aspects of the law of assault and battery should be emphasized. Not all touching is prohibited—only that type of

77

contact which is offensive and so should be discouraged in order
to lessen the chances of violence in our society. Thus, although
a person will be held liable for rude, potentially injurious, or
violent touchings, he will not be made to answer for gently
placing his hands on someone in an attempt to aid him, or for
any other contacts which are considered to be reasonable and
customary in the community. Where defendant intends to offensively touch a person but misses and makes contact with another person, he may be liable to that other person—intent to
offensively touch *someone* is enough to open him to liability.
Not only may defendant be found liable for personally touching plaintiff, but he also can be held responsible for setting an
object in motion (such as a stick or stone) which strikes
plaintiff. Defendant can be held liable for any resulting injuries
if he intended to make contact with the plaintiff in an offensive
manner—it is irrelevant that he did not intend to cause an injury—as where injury unexpectedly results from a pupil pushing
another down as a prank. In fact, since the essence of the law
of assault and battery is the protection from unwanted physical
contact, defendant may be held liable for an unwanted offensive
touching *even when plaintiff has sustained no physical injury*.

A defendant who is found liable for assault and battery must
pay an amount which the jury feels compensates plaintiff for
the indignity of being offensively touched, as well as for any
physical injury. In addition, where the assault and battery was
willful and malicious, the jury may award plaintiff "punitive"
damages—which are over and above plaintiff's actual injuries
—as a punishment to the defendant. Defendant may mitigate
the damages he is required to pay by showing that he was provoked into a willful attack by the words or acts of plaintiff.

A defendant may avoid liability in any one of three ways.
Firstly, he may prove that in fact he did not touch plaintiff in
an offensive manner as plaintiff claims. Secondly, he may show
that plaintiff consented to the offensive touching, and so should
not be allowed to complain in court. Examples of this occur
when plaintiff willingly enters into mutual combat with defendant, or agrees to participate in a dangerous game. Thirdly,
defendant may show that he was *justified* in making the offensive contact by an overriding social obligation. For example, a

policeman may show that his battery upon a person was justified by his duty to take into custody suspected felons. (It should be noted that it is *no* defense that defendant was insulted or provoked by plaintiff's words—mere words never justify an attack, no matter how harsh, loud, or insulting they may be— or that defendant has an uncontrollable temper, or that he was intoxicated.)

The defense of *justication* is very important to teachers, since much of their activity involves caring for, protecting, and, on occasion, punishing pupils. The following sections discuss the applicability of certain types of teacher activity to the defense of justification.

Corporal Punishment and Assault and Battery

As noted on page 76, in most states the teacher has the power to utilize corporal punishment. In other words, the teacher has a complete defense of *justification* to a suit by a pupil claiming assault and battery.

However, where he has abused his powers, the defense of justification will be lost and the teacher will be opened to civil and criminal liability for assault and battery. In the vast majority of states, this *in loco parentis* power will be lost where the teacher has acted in an unreasonable manner in applying the corporal punishment. The courts use four tests to determine the reasonableness of the teacher's action.

1) Was the regulation being enforced a reasonable one?
2) Was the form and extent of the force used reasonable in light of the type of offense committed by the pupil?
3) Was the form and extent of the force used reasonable in light of the pupil's age and known physical condition?
4) Did the teacher act without malice or personal ill will towards the pupil? (By definition, punishment based upon personal motives does not serve educational goals.)

If *any one* of these questions is answered in the negative by a court, the teacher will be exposed to liability. For example, a Texas case has ruled that it is not reasonable for a teacher to use his fists in administering punishment.

It should be noted that the infliction of a serious injury upon a pupil does not automatically create liability—it could have been the result of an accident or an unknown physical weakness—but such a dire result makes it very difficult for the teacher to persuade a court that the force used was reasonable in extent.

Although most of the statutes involving corporal punishment merely legislate the common law requirement of reasonableness, a few states have legislated variations of the general principles. In Delaware, Illinois and Oklahoma, teachers are given the same rights as parents to discipline pupils, and in Michigan, teachers are liable only for "gross abuse" in applying corporal punishment. Since parents are never sued by their offspring but are subject only to criminal prosecution for child abuse, and since the wording of the Michigan statute closely parallels language in child-abuse cases, it is assumed that the intention of these legislatures was to adapt the criminal standards of child-abuse cases to civil suits by pupils against teachers. That is, in these states a teacher being sued for damages by a pupil will not be held to a standard of reasonableness, but will have added protections just as if he were a criminal defendant: he may not be found liable for mere negligence, and he has the benefit of a presumption of good faith and correct discipline which the pupil-plaintiff must overcome. In order for the pupil in Delaware, Illinois, Oklahoma or Michigan to overcome the presumption in favor of the teacher and win his case he must prove that the punishment was administered:

1) so as to result in permanent injury; or
2) with malice, i.e., to gain revenge or vent hatred; or
3) so excessively as to be considered wanton and without just cause.

It should be noted that if the teacher has abused his authority, it is no defense that he was requested to be more strict or that the excessive punishment had good effect. Further, the teacher may be subject to criminal assault and battery charges.

Self-Defense and Defense of Others

The teacher has the same right as any citizen to protect his person from attack. When subjected to physical attack by a pupil, the teacher is justified in responding with such force as is reasonably necessary to end the threat. If the teacher responds with force which is excessive under the circumstances, or continues to use force after the pupil has submitted or attempts to flee, the teacher will lose the defense of justification in the event of an assault and battery suit.

The teacher's *in loco parentis* duty to protect pupils carries with it the concurrent right to use reasonable physical force to protect any of these pupils from physical attack. The teacher will not be held liable for a mistake as to who is the aggressor.

Medical Examination and Treatment

In every state the legislature has provided for the health protection of the school-age population by requiring immunization against certain diseases prior to any pupil's entering school. Further, school boards commonly are required to hire doctors and nurses to provide medical examinations at the onset of the school year and to test sight and hearing. Such provisions, although clearly impinging upon parental rights, are within the powers of the legislature to provide for the health and education of the state's citizens; however, absent such specific statutory authority, school personnel have *no* right to treat pupils in nonemergency situations, since such matters remain solely within the authority of the parents. The teacher may not provide first aid unless immediate attention is required to save the pupil from serious injury. In the absence of specific statutory authority, although a school may hire a nurse to detect pupil sickness, it cannot provide health care or medical treatment, require physical examinations, or take pupils to the hospital in nonemergency situations.

Search of Pupils

The average citizen has no right to search another person, and such an unconsented touching will result in assault and battery.

As discussed frequently in this book, the relationship between a teacher and pupil is such that the teacher has certain powers over a pupil which are not enjoyed by members of the general public. This is because the teacher is responsible for guiding the student's educational growth. The section on *Search of Desk or Locker,* pages 71–74, also applies to a search of the student's person. If the teacher stays within the rules outlined in that section, he will be safe in searching a pupil; however, if he strays outside the legal boundaries he will lose his justification and will be opened to liability for assault and battery.

Based upon a teacher's inherent rights to oversee the safety of his pupils, a teacher who discovers that a pupil is in possession of a dangerous weapon may use whatever force necessary to disarm him. This common law right has been enacted into statute in a few states.

9

Release of Information

Defamation Problems

A defamatory statement is a false communication made to a third party which tends to expose a person to hatred, contempt, or ridicule, or otherwise lower him in the estimation of the community. The purpose of the law of defamation is the protection of reputation. By way of example, the courts have found the following to be defamatory: a false accusation of mental impairment, unchastity, immoral sexual activity, or illegitimacy; an unfounded claim that a person has a loathsome disease; a false charge that a person is a thief or liar; and, name-calling which includes false imputations of socially unacceptable behavior, such as the claim that a person is "an interloper, a meddler and a spreader of distrust, discontent, and sedition," or a "disturber of the peace, quarrelsome, and a general nuisance." *The defamatory statement need only be communicated to one other person to be actionable;* it is "slander" if communicated orally, "libel" if spread in written form.

There are several defenses available to the person accused of defamation. Since the essence of the tort is the protection of reputation from false attacks, the defendant may avoid liability by showing the truth of his charges. Also, he may show that the complainant *invited* him to repeat the charges to another person. Further, although the courts will not strain to find a harmless meaning in the words used—they will normally read them in the "ordinary and popular sense"—defendant may escape liability by proving that in fact those listening or reading the communication did not accept it literally, but rather took it in its harmless sense. For example, witnesses to an argument may understand the accusation that someone is a "thief" to mean merely that he has done an unfair thing. Although it is not a complete defense, defendant may diminish the damages he is required to pay by showing that the plaintiff's reputation was already bad, or that defendant was provoked into the defamation by plaintiff's acts or insults. Finally, the defendant may show that he was *privileged* to make such statements without fear of liability.

In order to encourage citizens to fulfill their societal duties, in certain circumstances persons will not be held liable for making what would normally be defamatory statements.

> "Where a party makes a communication and such communication is prompted by a duty owed either to the public or to a third party, or the communication is one in which the party has an interest and it is made to another having a corresponding interest, the communication is privileged if made in good faith and without actual malice." *Zanley v. Hyde.*

The communication may involve a legal, moral, or social duty. For example, communications to the police or to public officials concerning matters within their responsibilities are privileged. Since educators are charged with the responsibility of controlling the learning environment in the public schools, communications involving school personnel are privileged to be protected from liability by this rule. It has been held that the privilege exists for communications by school personnel to parents or to the school board, or in letters to the newspapers concerning the administration of the schools; further, communications by parents to school personnel are privileged as are reports by psychologists to teachers.

Although this rule gives the teacher a certain amount of protection from suit, the privilege is *qualified;* that is, the insula-

tion from liability will be lost if the privilege is abused. Since the purpose of the privilege is to give educators protection from honest mistakes in the carrying out of their duties, it will be lost whenever the teacher's motives for acting are not grounded upon educational goals—whenever the teacher acts out of ill will towards a pupil, engages in a knowing lie, or is motivated by *any* reason other than the educational welfare of a student. Of course, the privilege will be lost if the subject matter of the communication goes beyond matter relevant to the educational process, as where a teacher discloses interesting—but educationally irrelevant—tidbits of information about a pupil's home life or out-of-school activities. It is also considered to be an abuse of the privilege to communicate the information to those who have no recognized social duty to deal with the problem. As one aspect of this, it should be noted that, although there are no cases involving teachers, cases in other areas of law make it clear that the teacher can lose the qualified privilege not only if he makes statements about a pupil to other pupils or non-school personnel but also if he discloses information to *those school personnel who do not have the responsibility of educating or counseling that pupil.*

In summary, teachers have a qualified privilege to communicate matters of educational significance to the proper school personnel. That is, they will be protected from liability if the information is later shown to be false and harmful to a pupil's reputation. However, the privilege will be lost if the teacher is motivated by personal reasons, if the subject matter goes beyond the bounds of educational relevancy, or if the teacher communicates the information to persons who are not involved in *that* pupil's education.

School Records

Records of county, city and township governmental units are public records, and as such are open to reasonable inspection by the public. This would allow the average citizen access to such things as school board minutes, enrollment figures and other gross statistics, written board and athletic association rules, written dress codes, etc.

Although there has been no case directly on point, it is likely that a pupil's school file is not considered to be a "public record" of the type discussed above. Going by general common law principles, it would seem that such a file would come under the heading of "quasi-public"—that is, it is open to inspection only by those who can show a special interest greater than that possessed by citizens generally. For example, a parent cannot be denied the right to see his child's record. This rule has been altered by statute in four states; California (available to police, school to which pupil is transferring, prospective employer—otherwise released only with parental permission); Delaware (available to government, police—released to another school or prospective employer only by consent of pupil or parent); Kentucky (academic records confidential and released only with parental consent); and New Jersey (pupils' records public).

For two reasons, it would seem that no one may require access to the personal notes of a teacher or counselor, where such personal papers do not become part of the student's file. Firstly, private papers of this sort are not considered "public records." Secondly, such notes may be "privileged communications" which are protected from disclosure in court (see the following section).

In the Courtroom

On occasion a teacher may be requested to testify in court concerning things which he has seen or heard about a pupil. All states recognize a right of "privileged communication" in the attorney-client relationship—neither party may divulge in court information gained because of the relationship—but only three states have recognized a similar right for school personnel.

The Michigan legislature has created a right of "privileged communication" in the teacher, similar to the traditional right of confidentiality in the attorney-client relationship. By law, the teacher may not be required—nor will he be permitted—to testify as to information gained by him in confidence.

> "No teacher, guidance officer, school executive or other professional person engaged in character building in the public schools or in any other educational institution, including any clerical worker of such schools and institutions, who maintains records in his custody, or who receives in confidence communications from students or other juveniles, shall be allowed in any proceedings, civil or criminal, in any court of this state, to disclose any information obtained by him from such records or such communications: nor to produce such records or transcript thereof, except that any such testimony may be given, with the consent of the person so confiding or to whom such records relate, if such person is 21 years of age or older, or, if such person is a minor, with the consent of his or her parent or legal guardian." *Mich. Comp. Laws Ann.* § 600.2165.

The statute does not affect testimony based upon nonconfidential sources, and so the teacher may testify as to information gained by personal observation or public communication. A similar statute was recently passed in Montana.

In North Dakota, those with "counselor" certificates have a similar privilege.

Although such a privilege obviously hinders the search for truth in the courtroom, it was created so as to accomplish a more important, day-to-day societal need—that of encouraging communication in a relationship of trust without fear of later courtroom disclosure, so that the teacher may better counsel the student.

Epilogue

How to Use This Book

IF you have read the foregoing chapters completely, you have absorbed the law of teacher-and-pupil as developed in over five hundred cases and several hundred statutes. Hopefully, it is clear by now that the teacher is not subject to vague and unpredictable legal dangers, but rather that the wealth of individual statutes and cases fit together into logical and coherent patterns which may be understood by the teacher and which may be utilized to solve new problems.

The first essential is that teachers stand *in loco parentis* in relation to their pupils. That is, they have rights and duties greater than those enjoyed by the general public but less than those retained by parents. On the one hand, the teacher has the right to exercise control over pupils with regards to their education: he may require them to follow reasonable rules, determine the manner in which they will spend their school hours, and punish them for conduct which is harmful to themselves, others, or the educational process.

On the other hand, the right to exercise such authority carries with it the concurrent responsibility for the protection of the pupils from injury to themselves or others due to their own immaturity and poor judgment. That is, by accepting the *in loco parentis* relationship the teacher is also accepting the duty

to refrain from being negligent in the care of his pupils. However, the courts have made it clear that the teacher does not
thereby become the insurer of the pupils' safety; he will not be
required to pay for every injury to a pupil, but merely will be
required to act reasonably in light of his responsibilities. Thus,
the many cases concerning recess, physical education, shop,
field trips, etc., should not be viewed as isolated decisions upon
the specific facts, but rather as brushstrokes which help to
paint the complete picture of the "reasonable teacher."

The reader must always bear in mind that the material
contained in this book deals solely with *legal liability*. That is,
it deals with the statutes and higher court decisions which
serve to allocate the burdens of paying for injuries and to de-
lineate the limits of power and authority in the school milieu.
As such, the legal do's and don'ts which you have just read
must not be taken as ethical or educational standards of the
profession. The laws establish the parameters, and it is up to
the teacher to decide which methods and procedures within
those legal boundaries provide the *best education* to the pupil.

Finally, this book is capable of being misused, to the teacher's detriment. It is not a cheap lawyer. It cannot analyze the
facts of a specific controversy, it cannot negotiate with the
other party, and it cannot stand up to the other party's lawyer.
If the teacher chooses to put this book on a shelf and not to
consult it until after an incident has occurred, then he has
squandered his chance to protect himself. Neither should the
teacher memorize isolated cases in order to cite them as "proof"
of the legality of a certain course of action, without looking to
the rationale and policies behind the remainder of the legal
authority in the field. Rather, this book should be used to sensi-
tize the teacher to trouble areas, so that he may spot problems
ahead of time and act to minimize the chance of suffering
legal liability. Therein lies the value and purpose of this book.

Appendix A

Glossary

No attempt is made to provide universal definitions for the legal terms in the following glossary. Rather, the definitions are intended to deal with those meanings relevant to the context of this book.

ACCIDENT. An unusual and unexpected occurrence, which may have been an "unavoidable accident" or the result of "negligence."

ACTIONABLE. That which will furnish legal grounds for an "action" (lawsuit).

ASSAULT. A threat of force, where the aggressor appears able to imminently carry out his threat.

ASSUMPTION OF RISK. The injured person is barred from recovering damages from another because he appreciated the nature and extent of the risk, and voluntarily subjected himself to it.

BATTERY. An unconsented, offensive touching of another person.

CAUSE IN FACT. An act or omission such that the accident would not have occurred but for that cause.

CIVIL LIABILITY. The result of a defendant losing a lawsuit in which plaintiff claimed that defendant injured him;

91

the payment of damages by a defendant to a plaintiff to compensate plaintiff for his injuries.

COMMON LAW.   The body of law which has been built up by the decisions of higher courts, as opposed to law created by the writing of statutes.

CONSTITUTION.   That document written when this country was formed which is the "highest law of the land" and, as such, supersedes any conflicting statutes or court decisions.

CONSTITUTIONAL RIGHT.   Something which a person is entitled to do or have, which is bestowed upon him by the Constitution of the United States; a right which may not be destroyed by legislation or court decision.

CONTRIBUTORY NEGLIGENCE.   The injured person is barred from recovering damages from another because an act or omission on the part of the injured person was not what a reasonably prudent person in the same circumstances would have done, and the act or omission contributed to his own injury; even though another person was negligent, the injured person cannot recover because his conduct did not meet up to the standard required for his own protection.

CORPORAL PUNISHMENT.   The use of physical force by a teacher for the purpose of maintaining proper discipline.

CRIMINAL LIABILITY.   Being found guilty in a criminal case; the punishment is a fine or prison sentence.

DEFAMATION.   A false statement which holds another person up to ridicule, hatred, or contempt, or otherwise lowers him in the estimation of the community.

DEFENDANT.   The person or corporation who is being sued.

DEFENSE.   A reason offered by defendant as to why he should not be made to pay for plaintiff's injury; it may be a denial of what plaintiff has claimed, a claim that plaintiff's own acts have barred him from recovering from defendant, or an excuse for defendant's acts.

DUTY.   Something which a person must do; an obligation imposed by the law.

EXPULSION. The permanent barring of a student from attending school.

HIGHER COURT. A court which hears appeals from the decisions of trial courts; a Court of Appeals or Supreme Court.

IN LOCO PARENTIS. Having the rights and duties of the parents; as applied to teachers, in loco parentis rights and duties extend only to matters designed to achieve educational goals.

INJURY. Harm done to a person's body, mind, reputation, etc.

JUSTIFICATION. A reason given by defendant as to why, even though he injured plaintiff, he should not be held liable, based upon a right given to him by the law.

LIABILITY. The obligation imposed upon a person by a court to pay for the damage or injury which another person has suffered.

LIBEL. Defamation communicated in written form.

MATTER OF LAW. Where the judge may rule upon the issue without the necessity of allowing the jury to decide it, since the determination of the issue is so obvious that reasonable men could not possibly differ.

MISDEMEANOR. A minor crime, which is punishable by a fine or a short jail sentence; a lesser crime than a felony.

NEGLIGENCE PER SE. Conduct which may be declared to be negligence without any argument or proof as to the surrounding circumstances, either because it violates a statute or because it is very obviously something which a reasonably prudent person would not do.

NEGLIGENT ACT OR OMISSION. The failure to do something which a reasonably prudent person would do under the circumstances, or the doing of something which a reasonably prudent person would not do under the circumstances.

OBSCENITY. Words or acts which are so vulgar and without redeeming social or political value that they fall outside the constitutional protection of "speech."

OMISSION. A failure to do something.

PLAINTIFF. The person or corporation who is suing another, who claims to have been illegally injured by the defendant.

POWER. The legal ability to prescribe rules and punish others for breaking those rules.

PRIVILEGE. A benefit held by a group beyond the common advantages of ordinary citizens which, as such, is subject to being forfeited if abused; a reason based upon an overriding social duty as to why defendant should not be made to compensate plaintiff, even though defendant injured plaintiff.

PRIVILEGED COMMUNICATION. A private communication which is protected from being disclosed in court.

PROXIMATE CAUSE. An act or omission which, in a natural and continuous sequence, unbroken by any new, independent cause, produced the injury complained of, without which the injury would not have occurred; in practice, a cause which is sufficiently closely related to the injury complained of to warrant making the actor pay for it.

QUALIFIED PRIVILEGE. A privilege which is forfeited if abused.

REASONABLY PRUDENT PERSON. That person who acts with due care for his safety and the safety of others, doing only that which will not subject himself or others to an unreasonable risk of injury; it is a negligent act or omission to fail to act as a reasonably prudent person would under the circumstances.

RIGHT. Something which, by law, a person is entitled to do or have.

SEARCH WARRANT. A paper issued by a judge which authorizes the police to search a person or a specific area of a house or building, based upon the sworn belief of the police that illegal items are probably there.

SLANDER. Defamation communicated orally.

SUSPENSION. The barring of a student from attending school for a limited period of time, after which he may return to school.

TORT. A legal wrong committed upon a person or property independent of contract.

UNAVOIDABLE ACCIDENT. Harm which is not intended and
which, under the circumstances, could not have been
foreseen and prevented by the exercise of reasonable
care; harm for which no one must pay damages to the
injured person.

VERDICT. Where there is a jury, a decision by the jury concerning the facts submitted to it; where there is no jury,
the decision by the judge regarding the issues of the
case.

Appendix B

Statutory and Judicial Authority

CHAPTER ONE: THIS BOOK—WHAT AND WHY

States where Boards of Education pay pupils' damage awards: Arizona (*Stone*), California, Connecticut, Illinois, Louisiana, Massachusetts, Nevada, New Mexico, New York, North Carolina, North Dakota, Oregon (only when the school board has insurance, *Vendrell*), Washington, Wisconsin, Wyoming.
Principal is head teacher: *White* v. *State*.

CHAPTER TWO: THE ELEMENTS OF A SUIT FOR NEGLIGENCE

Duty

Doctor has no duty to render first aid: *Hurley*.
No duty to rescue a drowning man: *Osterlind*.
Must supervise pupils' activities: *Briscoe, McLeod*.
Must warn them of known dangers: *Eastman, McDonell*.
Must protect pupils from themselves: *Kidwell, Ridge*.
Must protect pupils from each other: *Buzzard, Lilienthal Marques, McLeod, Station*.

Must disarm pupils: *Christofides.*
Must stop fights: *Charonnat, Cianci.*
Must summon first aid: *Mogahgab,* 1961–62 Mich. Att. Gen. 419
(No. 4061). Cf., *Duda, Jarrett, Pirkle, Szabo, Welch.*

Negligent Act or Omission

Not liable merely because an accident occurred: *Doktor, Ford, Gain-cott, Greathouse.*

Ideal citizen with same physical characteristics and special skills as defendant: *Jakubiec.*

Person with average intelligence and even temperament: *Deisentieter.*

Cannot claim less than average intelligence: *Lillibridge.*

Take into account teacher's responsibilities towards pupils: *Gaincott* (reasonable care "tested in the light of the existing relationship").

Law does not require that the exact hazard be foreseen (quote): *Comstock,* p. 636.

Need only foresee some kind of harm: *Charonnat* (inadequate playground supervision), *Drum* (pencil thrown by teacher), *Haymes* (dark coatroom), *Jones v. Jones* (hot bowl of soup near two-year-old), *Kidwell* (upright piano with keyboard towards wall), *Lilienthal* (flipped jackknife).

If not reasonably foreseeable, it is an "unavoidable accident": *Chimerofsky, Ferreira* (student acting in play uses real bullet), *Gaincott, McLaren, West.*

Presence of children makes chances of accident more likely: *Buttrick.* Cf., *Huff.*

Not foreseeable that pupil with water bottle would fall off chair: *Gaincott.*

Foreseeable that pupil carrying books would develop heart trouble: *Feuerstein.*

Illinois and Texas statutes—no liability for mere negligence in discretionary acts: 85 Ill. Stat. Ann. § 2-201, Tex. 1971 session Laws, ch. 830.

Illinois—liable only for "willful and wanton negligence" with regards to acts which require professional judgment: *Woodman.*

Illinois—decision to allow aggressive pupil on basketball team is discretionary: *Fustin.*

Illinois—amount of pupil movement about classroom is discretionary: *Woodman.*

Illinois—for experiment explosion need only show negligence: *Kaske.*

Injury

Must pay for any injuries directly resulting from wrongful act: *Webster, Woodyard.*

Must pay for any subsequent reinjury: *Campbell, Stahl.*

Liable for diseases acquired as a result of lowered defenses: *Beauchamp, Furtado* (cancer).

Must pay for harm done by negligent medical treatment: *Thompson.*

Liable for injuries due to emotional shock: *Halton, Purcell.*

Close Connection Between the Negligent Act or Omission and the Injury

No liability where child climbed *over* the fence: *McLendon.*

No liability where boys bumped heads in course of game: *Kaufman, Kerby.* See also, *Wright* v. *City of San Bernardino High School District.*

Proximate cause if acted in natural and continuous sequence, unbroken by independent cause: *Weissert.*

Motorist liable for fallen canopy: *Parks.*

Liable for negligent installation of lightning rod: *White* v. *Schnoebelen.*

Auto manufacturer liable for faulty brakes even though driver knew of them: *Comstock.* Cf., *Wamser* (contractor held liable for the negligent placement of an angle iron even though it was knocked down by another person).

Teacher liable where negligence creates a dangerous situation upon which a pupil negligently acts to injure another: *DeBenedittis, Marques, Rodriguez, Station.*

Liable if absence led to rowdy and dangerous play: *Briscoe* ("keep away" football), *Cirillo* (same), *Dailey* (slap boxing), *Decker* (jumping from bleachers), *Gattavara* (playing near driveway), *Lopez* (standing on swing), *Ogando* (using glass doors as a base), *Raymond* (running alongside bus in an attempt to be the first one on), *Tymkowicz* (playing "blackout").

Liable if pupils are left exposed to a dangerous situation: *Marques* (discus throwing practice), *Miller* v. *Board of Education* (entry through defective door onto fire escape), *Rose* (burning tree stump). Cf., *Huff* (burning trash).

Not liable if the injury was due to a sudden act: *Butler* (throwing printing type), *Conway* (push), *McDonell* (running into passerby), *Ohman* (throwing pencil), *Pollard* (quickly raising fence

wire), *Segerman* (accidental kick while doing exercises), *Woodsmall* (playful push).
Railroad not liable where fire started by bystander: *Watson.*
Teacher liable for attack by pupil upon other, in absence of supervision: *Beck* (assault), *Christofides* (stabbing after wielding knife 5–10 minutes), *Gonzales* (throwing pointer after long argument), *Nash* (poke in eye after teasing), *Silverman* (playground assault), *Titus* (shooting paper clips).
Liable for injuries due to fight, in absence of supervision: *Charonnat, Cianci, Forgnone.*
Liable for rape, in absence of supervision: *McLeod.*
Not liable where malicious act was sudden and without warning: *Chmela, Guiten, McDonell.*

CHAPTER THREE: DEFENSES TO A
SUIT FOR NEGLIGENCE

Most governmental bodies enjoy immunity from suit: e.g., *Daniels, Mokovich, Sayers* v. *School District, Williams* v. *Primary School District.*
Employees of governmental agencies are not personally immune from suit: *Duncan, Gaincott.*
In most states the teacher must pay damages: Alabama, Alaska, Arkansas, Colorado, Delaware, District of Columbia, Florida, Georgia, Hawaii, Idaho, Indiana, Iowa, Kansas, Kentucky, Maine, Maryland, Michigan, Minnesota, Mississippi, Missouri, Montana, Nebraska, New Hampshire, New Jersey, Ohio, Oklahoma, Pennsylvania, Rhode Island, South Carolina, South Dakota, Tennessee, Texas, Utah, Vermont, Virginia, West Virginia.
In some states the school district will bear the loss: Arizona (*Stone*), California, Connecticut, Illinois, Louisiana, Massachusetts, Nevada, New Mexico, New York, North Carolina, North Dakota, Oregon (only if the school board has insurance, *Vendrell*), Washington, Wisconsin, Wyoming.
Assumption of risk is similar to contributory negligence: Some. state courts have found the difference between assumption of risk and contributory negligence to be so meaningless when applied to actual situations that they have ordered the abandonment of the former entirely, e.g., Michigan (*Felgner*).

Judge will almost never rule a child to be contributorily negligent as a matter of law: e.g., *Ross*.

Child is held to the standard of a reasonable child of his age, capacity, and experience: *Clemens, DeNoyer, Harris* v. *Crawley.*

In many states, very young children cannot be found contributorily negligent: e.g., in Michigan, children under seven. *Baker* v. *Alt., Queen Ins. Co.*

Juries finding no contributory negligence: *Decker* (jumping off bleachers), *Gattavara* (backing out of doorway onto driveway), *Hutchins* (attempting to cross a pit on a plank), *Raymond* (running alongside bus), *Taylor* v. *Oakland Scavenger Co.* (15-year-old dashing across street). Cf., *Dutcher* (welding near gas tank).

Students learning the use of machines are expected to operate them imperfectly: *Rodriguez.*

Pupil is more likely to be exonerated when the teacher has requested him to take part in the activity: *Bellman* (tumbling), *Feuerstein* (carrying heavy books), *Keesee* (soccer), *Lee* v. *Board of Education* (playing in street).

. . . where the teacher has set a negligent example: *Rodriguez, Rook.*

. . . where the activity is almost customary: *Briscoe* ("keep away" football), *Satarino* (running across street to athletic fields), *Taylor* v. *Oakland Scavenger Co.* (same).

. . . where the teacher failed to provide safety instructions: *Ahern* (power saw without guard), *Engel* (rockets), *Ridge* (power saw without guard).

. . . where the pupil was attracted to an interesting place: *Huff* (burning trash), *Swartley* (lumber storeroom).

. . . where the pupil was attracted to an interesting activity: *Engel* (rockets).

Permission note is not a consent to negligence: *Swartley,* 1938 Wis. Att. Gen. (Dec. 27, 1938).

Parent cannot sign away the rights of a child: *Farah,* 28 Conn. Att. Gen. 245 (1954), 1938 Wis. Att. Gen. (Dec. 27, 1938).

CHAPTER FOUR: SUPERVISION ON THE SCHOOL GROUNDS

Recess

May not supervise playground activities while in building: *Lopez.*

. . . even if the teacher is watching through a window: *Miller* v. *Board of Education.*

It is no excuse to be doing other tasks: *Briscoe* (holding make-up class), *Decker* (supervising in another area), *Silverman* (collecting playground equipment).

Dangerous situations must be supervised: *Satarino* (crossing street), *Taylor* v. *Oakland Scavenger Co.* (crossing street). Cf. *Rose* (burning trash).

Supervisors must be qualified: *Garber* (janitor not suitable supervisor for noon recess).

Up to Jury as to whether the number of supervisors was adequate: *Charonnat, Rodrigues, Silverman.*

Liable for injuries due to roughhouse games or dangerous situations, in the absence of adequate supervision: *Briscoe* ("keep-away"), *Dailey* ("slap boxing"), *Gattavara* (playing near driveway), *Lopez* (standing on swings), *Miller* v. *Board of Education* (standing on fire escape), *Tymkowicz* ("blackout").

Liable for malicious acts which are not sudden, in absence of adequate supervision: *Beck* (assault), *Cianci* (fight), *McLeod* (rape).

Not liable for sudden and unexpected acts: *Kaufman* (bumped heads while playing basketball), *McDonell* (ran into passerby), *Woodsmall* (sudden playful push).

Teacher need not inspect playground equipment: *Medsker*. Neither do the pupils have a duty to inspect the equipment before they play on it: *Kelley*.

Must warn pupils of dangerous conditions of which the teacher is aware: *Eastman*. Same for the classroom: *Haymes*.

Must enforce play rules: *Buzzard* (no bike riding on playground), *Germond* (handing out baseball bats).

Must break up fights: *Charonnat*. Cf., *Dailey* ("slap boxing").

Must not lead children in dangerous games: *Davis* v. *Gavalas, Lee* v. *Board of Education* (playing on school roadway), *Rook* (blanket toss, with torn blanket).

In absence of negligence, not liable for unavoidable accidents: *Ford, Nestor, Woodsmall.*

Need not know what each pupil is doing as long as supervision is provided: *Ford, Woodsmall.*

Need not stop activity because of outside chance of injury: *Chimerofsky* (use of playground equipment), *Kerby* (basketball), *Nestor* (baseball), *Pirkle* (closely supervised touch football game), *Rodrigues* (use of playground equipment), *Wire* (jump rope).

Must supervise pupils on ground for lunch: *Dailey, Decker, Forgnone, Ogando.*

Must supervise pupils gathering in communal areas between exams: *Cianci.*

Before and After School

No supervision necessary on grounds prior to class time: *Berner.*

No supervision required when pupils are leaving school or returning: *Lawes, Leibowitz.*

No supervision needed when pupils remain after school to work on projects: *Tannenbaum.*

No supervision necessary when pupils remain after school to play on the playground: *Bennett, Chimerofsky.*

Supervision is required where trash is burned on the grounds: *Huff.*

Supervision necessary where icy conditions make snowballing dangerous: *Cioffi.* Cf., *Lawes.*

School-sponsored carnival must be supervised: *Beck.*

Must supervise pupils waiting for buses on school grounds: *Nash, Raymond, Selleck, Titus.*

School wrestling matches must be supervised: *Carabba.*

After-school shop activities must be supervised: cf., *Ross.*

After-school laboratory activities must be supervised: cf., *Brigham Young.*

Still no duty of supervision when students mill about on school grounds prior to class in the morning and after lunch: *Berner, Lawes.*

. . . but there is some judicial impatience with this rule: Dissent in *Lawes.*

No supervision required while pupil is going to and from school: *Gilbert, Kerwin.* Although the teacher has no *duty* to provide supervision, he has the *right* to make rules concerning pupil safety if he wishes. *Kerwin.*

Supervision necessary for school-sponsored activities: *Beck* (carnival), *Lehmuth* (parade).

Hallways

No ongoing duty of hallway supervision: *Chmela, Reithardt, Sanchick.*

Must supervise hallways if it is known that pupils are rowdy: cf., *Chmela, Sanchick.*

Ongoing rowdiness not proved by a few prior instances: cf., *Gallagher.*

No duty of supervision before the start of classes: *Berner.*

No duty of supervision after school: *Leibowitz.* Cf., *Tannenbaum.*

No duty to accompany pupils to the lavatory: *Baughn.*

Must remedy violations of rules: cf., *Buzzard, Charonnat*.
Need not intervene in harmless horseplay: *Doktor*.

First Aid

Citizen owes no duty to summon doctor or provide first aid: *Hurley, Osterlind*.

Teacher has authority to render first aid: *Jarrett*.

Teacher must call a doctor in emergency if parent cannot be reached: *Mogahgab*, 1961–62 Mich. Att. Gen. 419 (No. 4061). Cf., *Duda, Szabo, Welch* v. *Dunsmuir Joint Union High School District*.

Teacher must give first aid if not one second can be wasted: 1961–62 Mich. Att. Gen. 419 (No. 4061).

Must cease first aid when the doctor arrives: *Welch* v. *Dunsmuir Joint Union High School District*.

Not an "emergency" unless serious injury is an immediate threat: *Moss, Tabor*.

In California, teacher may apply "reasonable medical treatment": Cal. Educ. Code § 11709.

In an emergency, first aid may be applied even over the objection of a pupil: *Ollet*.

Liable if first aid which a reasonable teacher should know is unwise or medically unsound is applied: *Guerrieri* (holding pupil's finger in scalding water for 10 minutes), *Mogahgab, Welch* v. *Dunsmuir Joint Union High School District* (moving player with back injury to sidelines, instead of bringing doctor on sidelines to player).

If it is not an emergency, teacher need not summon first aid: *Duda, Guerrieri*.

Non-Teachers

School board may hire aides under general authority to hire personnel: 1956 Mich. Att. Gen. 228 (No. 3647).

Non-teachers cannot supervise "dangerous" gym activities: *Bellman, Brittan, Gardner*.

Janitor is not a suitable supervisor: *Garber*.

Non-teacher who cannot control class may not be left alone with the pupils: cf., *Hendrickson, Mitchell* v. *Churches*.

CHAPTER FIVE: SUPERVISION OF THE CLASS

Classroom Supervision

Teacher is liable if he allows a dangerous situation to exist: *Haymes.*
Teacher not automatically liable for injuries occurring in his absence: *Cirillo; Segerman.*
No liability of injury is due to sudden act: *Briscoe, Doktor, Guyten, Nash, Ohman, Pollard, Rodrigues, Woodsmall.*
Injuries suffered as a result of a build-up of rowdyism will result in liability: *Christofides* (flashing knife for 5–10 minutes), *Gonzales* (10 minute argument).
There is a duty to break up fights: *Charonnat.*
Not required to intervene in seemingly harmless horseplay: *Doktor, Sanchick.* Cf., *Berner.*
Required to take reasonable precautions with known violent or aggressive pupils: *Ferraro, Weiner.*
What are reasonable precautions depends upon the situation: *Weiner.*
Even with a known violent pupil, not liable for sudden acts which a teacher could not have prevented: *Bertola.*
Liable if teacher fails to warn a substitute: *Ferraro.*

Shop and Laboratory

Must instruct as to degree of danger and gravity of possible injury: *Crabbe, Reagh, Ridge, Ross.*
Must detail dangers of putting inappropriate objects into machines: *Rodriguez* (manually aiding bowling pinsetting machinery), *Ross* (buffing rings which were attached to pliable leather straps).
Must instruct as to the proper use of a dangerous instrumentality: *Calandri* (cannon), *Engel* (rockets). Although it would seem to be negligent even to encourage such activities, no case has yet dealt with the issue.
Must do more than rely on text instructions: *Brigham Young, Station.*
Must instruct (quote): *Mastrangelo*, page 636.
Teacher must set a good example: *Rodriguez.*
In many cases the teacher claims adequate instruction, the pupil says no: *Ahern, Henry, Klenzendorf.*
Must make sure that those with educational difficulties understand: *Rodriguez.*

Responsibility to provide suitable equipment is with the Board of Education: *Banks* v. *Seattle School District.*

Teacher must withhold equipment which he should know is defective: *Crabbe.*

Teacher responsible for replacing broken or missing equipment: *Rodriguez* (protective screens), *Ross* (goggles).

Teacher must choose that piece of equipment suitable for the job at hand: *Maede* (teacher gave pupil wrong oxygen gauge for welder).

Statutes which require eye protective devices: 52 Ala. Code § 1(12), Ariz. Rev. Stat. § 15-1501, Ark. Stat. Ann. § 80-1634, Cal. Educ. Code § 1290, Conn. Gen. Stat. Ann. § 10-214a (school board may make regulations), Del. Stat. § 14-8301, 122 Ill. Stat. Ann. § 698.11, Ind. Stat. Ann. § 28-5724, Kan. Stat. Ann. § 72-5388, 77 Md. Code Ann. § 89, Mass. Rev. Stat. § 71-55c, Minn. Stat. Ann. § 126.20, N.C. Gen. Stat. § 115-258, Ohio Rev. Code § 3313.643, 70 Okla. Stat. Supp. 1969 § 601, 24 Pa. Stat. Ann. § 5301, R.I. Gen. Laws § 16-21-15, S.C. Code § 32-697, S.D. Comp. Laws § 13-24-18.2, Tenn. Code Ann. § 49-4401, Texas Educ. Code § 21.909, Utah Code Ann. § 53-1-20, Va. Code § 22-10.2, Wash. Rev. Code Ann. App. 70.6 § 2, Wyo. Stat. § 21.1-183.

The statute implies liability if the teacher does not enforce it: cf., *Rodriguez, Rook.*

Negligence to shelve unlabeled, uncorked acid: *Grosso, Station* (alcohol).

Dangerous machines should be locked when not in use: *DeBenedittis.*

Storage areas must be safe: *Swartley.*

Not liable when students pilfer chemicals to use outside of class: *Frace, Gregory, Hutchison, Moore* v. *Order Minor Conventuals, Reagh, Wilhelm.*

Teacher should not pit students against each other when performing dangerous activities: *Rodriguez* (working with machinery).

Negligent teacher not insulated from liability by later negligent act of pupil: *DeBenedittis, Rodriguez, Station.*

Liable for failure to provide protective screens: *Rodriguez.*

Not liable if working conditions are safe: *Goodman, Gregory, Morris* v. *Ortiz.*

Not liable for injury due to sudden unexpected acts: *Morris* v. *Ortiz, Meyer, Taylor* v. *Kelvin.*

Liable for explosion of demonstration experiment: *Damsgaard, Kaske.*

Liable if equipment is dropped onto pupil: *Furtado.*

Physical Education

Teacher owes reasonable care in supervision and instruction: *Marques, Stehn.*

Teacher not liable for injury where he has acted reasonably in making conditions safe: *Cambareri* (mat slip), *Ellis* (collision while playing tag), *Kerby* (unknown physical defect), *Ostrowski* (strained knee), *Turner* (spectator near sidelines), *Vendrell* (pupil did not understand instructions, but did not come forward to ask for clarification).

Liable for injuries as a result of roughhouse play: *Cirillo.*

Liable for injuries due to a dangerous situation: *Marques* (students playing in discus practice area).

Not liable for injuries due to sudden, unexpected acts: *Wright* v. *City of San Bernardino* (thrown ball), *Segerman* (accidental kick).

Must adequately instruct in the athletic activity: *Bellman, Clark, Gardner, LaValley, Sayers* v. *Ranger, Stehn.*

May not assign exercises which are too advanced: *Bellman, Brooks, Govel, Keesee.*

Liable for aggravation of known injuries: *Cherney* (pupil complained about weak wrists), *Luce, Morris* v. *Union High School District.*

Mats should be properly placed: *Fein, Govel.*

Bases must be secured to floor: *Bard.*

Sharp projections must be padded: *Bradley.*

Overcrowding of play area must be prevented: *Bauer.*

Spectators should be kept out of the way of players: *Domino, Marques.*

Must supervise street crossing: *Satarino, Taylor* v. *Oakland Scavenger Co.*

Must not permit the students to use equipment which the teacher knows or should know is defective: *Adams.*

Not liable for unforeseen equipment failures: *Quigley* (stall bars came loose).

Sports which are not considered "dangerous": *Ellis* (tag), *Pirkle* (touch football, when played by skilled participants), *Wright* v. *City of San Bernardino* (handball or tennis).

Sports considered to be "dangerous": *Bellman* (dive and roll over two pupils), *Brooks* (soccer), *Keesee* (soccer), *LaValley* (boxing), *Reynolds* (wrestling).

One court found headstands to be a "dangerous" activity: *Gardner.*

Use of physical fitness testing devices requires added care: *Brittan.*

Instruction by advanced students not acceptable for "dangerous" activity: *Bellman, Brittan.*

Instruction by student-teacher not acceptable for "dangerous" activity: *Gardner.*

When playing a "dangerous" sport, pupils must compete only against those of similar size: *Brooks.* Cf., *Keesee, Reynolds.*

Match-up need not be exact: *Reynolds.*

No requirement of size match-up for "nondangerous" sports: *Ellis, Pirkle.*

CHAPTER SIX: THE TEACHER'S RESPONSIBILITIES DURING SCHOOL-SPONSORED ACTIVITIES

Safety Patrol

By statute, school and teacher are immune to suit for injuries arising out of safety patrol activity: Alaska Stat. §§ 14.33.010,-.030, -.060, Ark. Stat. Ann. § 80-4401,-02,-04, 85 Ill. Stat. Ann. § 211 and 122 Ill. Stat. Ann. § 10-22.28, Minn. Stat. Ann. § 126.15, Mont. Rev. Codes § 75-8310, N.J. Stat. Ann. § 18A:42-1, N.Y. Educ. Law § 806, Utah Code § 53-12-1, 16 Vt. Stat. Ann. § 1482, Wis. Stat. Ann. § 40.63.

Some statutes authorize safety patrols, with the liability resting on the Boards of Education: Cal. Educ. Code § 12051, Idaho Code §§ 33-1801,-1802 (teacher indemnified by school board insurance), Nev. Rev. Stat. § 616.075, Ore. Rev. Stat. § 336.460, Wash. Rev. Code Ann § 46.61.385.

Safety patrol supervisors are merely required to act reasonably: Even where one has no duty to provide for another's safety, if one decides to provide help a duty arises to act carefully. *Kotarski, Raymond.* Cf., *Teall.*

Liable if guard is not adequately instructed: cf., *Brigham Young, Ferraro, Rodriguez.*

Liable if guard is physically unfit: cf., *Davis* v. *Gavales.*

Liable if guard is emotionally unsuitable: cf., *Mitchell* v. *Churches, Rounds, Zuckerberg.*

Teacher should realize that others will rely: cf., *Teall* (city held liable for a dangerous traffic light arrangement, since the public relies upon such aids to protect, not endanger, their safety).

Supervisor will not be liable merely because an accident occurred: cf., *Ragonese.*

In three states pupils are authorized by statute to direct traffic: Cal.

Educ. Code § 12055, Idaho Code § 33-1801, Wash. Rev. Code Ann. § 46.61.385.

School is not *required* to provide a safety patrol: 1959–60 Mich. Att. Gen. 757 (No. 2610).

Field Trips

Not liable for injuries due to sudden, unexpected acts: *Arnold.*

Not required to inspect school vehicle: *Adams.*

Will not be held liable if teacher has acted reasonably as to pupils' safety: *Adams, Arnold.*

Permission slip is not a consent to negligence: *Swartley,* 1938 Wis. Att. Gen. (Dec. 27, 1938).

Parent cannot sign away his child's rights: *Farah,* 28 Conn. Att. Gen. 245 (1954), 1938 Wis. Att. Gen. (Dec. 27, 1938).

Must be more vigilant if chances of injury are greater: cf., *Buttrick, Huff, Rodriguez, Swartley.*

Interscholastic Athletics

Spectators must be kept out of the way of the players: *Domino, Marques.*

Not liable to spectator who enters a restricted area, or who is so ignorant as to wander into an obviously dangerous playing area: *Turner.*

Not liable for every injury suffered while traveling: *Adams.* Cf., *Arnold.*

Need not inspect school-supplied vehicle: *Arnold.*

Can make reasonable rules for athletes: e.g., *Board of Directors* v. *Green* (school board), *Marino* (athletic association), *Neuhaus* (coach).

School-sponsored Events

School must supervise school-sponsored events: *Beck* (carnival), *Lehmuth* (parade).

Counseling

No right to presence of attorney at counseling session: *Madera.*

CHAPTER SEVEN: THE ENFORCEMENT OF SCHOOL RULES

Pupils must accept reasonable school rules: *Tanton,* 1929–30 Mich. Att. Gen. 412.

Teachers are *in loco parentis* in school-related matters: *Gaincott, People* v. *Jackson.*

Parents may be brought to account for abusing their rights to discipline their children: e.g., *People* v. *Green.*

What Conduct May Be Regulated

May punish pupils who are tardy: *Burdick, Fertich*, 1929–30 Mich. Att. Gen. 412.

. . . truant: *Burdick, Davis* v. *Ann Arbor Public Schools.*

. . . smoke on school grounds in violation of rules: 8 Wis. Att. Gen. 110 (1919).

. . . cheat on examinations: cf., *Barker, Goldberg, Goldwyn.*

. . . disrupt others: *Davis* v. *Ann Arbor Public Schools, Farrell* v. *Joel.*

. . . fail to hand in homework: *Balding.*

. . . hand in someone else's work: *Samuel Benedict Memorial School.*

. . . come to class unprepared: *Sewell, Thomason* (refusal to do the classwork).

. . . fight in the halls: *Suits.*

. . . act insolently: *Byrd.*

. . . use profanity: *Baker* v. *Downey City Board of Education, Board of Education* v. *Helston, Brown* v. *Greer.*

. . . insult the teacher: *Board of Education* v. *Booth, Davis* v. *Ann Arbor Public Schools, Peck, Samuel Benedict Memorial School, Suits.*

. . . strike the teacher: *Brown* v. *Greer.*

. . . engage in malicious destruction of property: cf., *Davis* v. *Ann Arbor Public Schools, Holman, Perkins.*

Pupils may be required to follow reasonable classroom procedures: *Wulff.*

May require students to stay out of the teacher's effects: *Stevens* (teacher's chair), 1930–32 La. Att. Gen. 441 (private papers).

May ban noisy and disruptive heel plates: *Stromberg.* See pages 64–65 for a complete discussion of the school's rights to regulate the grooming of pupils.

May require proper attire at graduation ceremonies: *Valentine.* A pupil who refuses to wear proper attire may be prevented from taking part in the ceremonies, but his credits and diploma have been earned and so may not be withheld. *State ex rel. Roberts.*

Pupils must name which other students are breaking the rules: *Board of Education* v. *Helston.*

May require pupils to remain on the school grounds during lunchtime:

Bozeman, Casey County Board of Education, Fitzpatrick, Flory, Richardson. The exception is Hawaii. Haw. Rev. Stat. § 298-14.

May bar students from other schools, or non-students: *Banks* v. *Board of Public Instruction.*

Pupil receiving insufficient grades may be denied graduation: *Sweitzer* (even if he takes part in the ceremony).

School can regulate autos: e.g., Mich. Comp. Laws Ann. § 257.961 (on the grounds), 1960 Mich. Att. Gen. 51 (No. 3493) (on surrounding streets).

May prohibit pupils from driving to school altogether: 1963 Ky. Att. Gen. 486, 1960 Mich. Att. Gen. 51 (No. 3493). However, the school has no right to take away a student's drivers license. 1957 Fla. Att. Gen. 057-388 (Dec. 17, 1957).

Pupil may be punished even where his parent has ordered him to disobey a school rule: *Casey County Board of Education, Flory, Stromberg.*

Married students may be barred from nonacademic activities: *Board of Directors* v. *Green, Cochrane* v. *Board of Education* (split decision), *Estay, Kissick, State ex rel. Baker.*

A pupil may not be suspended merely for being married: *Board of Education* v. *Bentley, Carrollton-Farmers Branch Independent School District.*

Teacher's authority extends to all pupils in the school: *Appeal of School District of Borough of Old Forge.*

Rules need only be sufficiently precise so that the standards are understood: *Banks* v. *Board of Public Instruction.*

Teacher may make reasonable rules: *Deskins, State ex rel. Burpee, Wulff,* Idaho Code § 33-1224.

Some rules are so basic that the teacher need not bother to state them: *Brown* v. *Greer, Hasson, State ex rel. Burpee, State ex rel. Dresser.*

School has inherent power to regulate pupil conduct to and from school: *Deskins, Hutton.*

Some states have statutes expressly authorizing the school to regulate pupil conduct en route to and from school: Ariz. Rev. Stat. § 15-201, Cal. Educ. Code § 13557, Ky. Rev. Stat. Ann. § 161.180, La. Rev. Stat. Ann. § 17-416, Mich. Comp. Laws Ann. § 340.614, Miss. Code Ann. § 6282-24, Mont. Rev. Codes § 75-6310, Nev. Rev. Stat. § 392.460, N.J. Stat. Ann. § 18A:25-2, 24 Pa. Stat. Ann. § 13-1317, Wash. Rev. Code Ann. § 28.67.100.

May require pupils to go straight home after school: *Jones* v. *Cody.*

May require pupils to refrain from fighting while en route: *Deskins, Hutton.*

No duty to provide supervision en route: *Kerwin,* Nev. Rev. Stat. §
392.460.

Criterion for punishment for off-school acts is whether the conduct is
deleterious to the pupils: *Douglas, Lander, O'Rourke, Tanton.*

Power to punish for acts outside of school hours is essential (quote):
State ex rel. Dresser, page 235.

May punish for nighttime destruction of school property: *Board of
Education* v. *Hansen.*

May punish a pupil for calling the teacher names in front of other
pupils: *Lander.*

May punish for public defiance of disciplinary procedures: *Goldberg,
Tanton.*

May punish for abusing other children: *O'Rourke.* The trial judge
specifically found that the pupil's bullying was demoralizing the
other pupils in the school.

May suspend on the basis of out-of-school acts which raise fears as
to the safety of members of the class if the pupil is allowed to
attend school: *R.R.*

Older cases—can punish for out-of-school immoral conduct: *Douglas*
(drunk downtown), *Tanton* (brazen female student).

May ban school-connected organizations to promote safety: *Kinzer*
(may ban high school football and punish those who organized
a weekend team which purported to represent the school), *State
ex rel. Evans.*

. . . encourage concentration upon academics: *Brown* v. *Wells.*

. . . protect against bad influences: *Estay, Marino.*

Interscholastic athletics is a privilege, not a right: *Kinzer, Marino,
State ex rel. Evans, Tennessee Secondary School Athletic Association.*

May place reasonable restrictions upon athletic participation: *Brown*
v. *Wells* (pupils who play on other organized teams or who play
off-season are not eligible), *Board of Education* v. *Green, Estay,
Marino* (school transfer rules), *Mitchell* v. *Louisiana High
School Athletic Association* (lose one year of eligibility if volun-
tarily repeat a grade), *Sanders* v. *Louisiana High School Athletic
Association, Scott* v. *Kilpatrick* (eligibility rules), *State ex rel.
Indiana High School Athletic Association* (same), *Tennessee
Secondary School Athletic Association* (same).

. . . even if a scholarship is lost: *Estay, Sanders.*

Athletes may be held to stricter standards of conduct as a condition
for being on the team: *O'Connor* (taking away school "letter"
for drinking beer off school grounds).

Married students may be barred from athletics: *Board of Directors* v. *Green, Cochrane* v. *Board of Education* (split decision), *Estay, Kissick, State ex rel. Baker.*

Inherent right to regulate fraternities and sororities: *Coggins, Holroyd, Lee* v. *Hoffman, Nicholls, Passel.*

Statutes in some states prohibit fraternities and sororities completely: Ark. Stat. Ann. § 80-2003, Cal. Educ. Code § 10604, Fla. Stat. Ann. § 232.40, Idaho § 33-1901, 122 Ill. Stat. Ann. § 31-2 (school board *shall* suspend violators, § 31-3), Ind. Stat. Ann. § 28-6105, Iowa Code Ann. § 287.1, Kan. Stat. Ann. § 72-5311, 20 Maine Rev. Stat. Ann. § 803, Mich. Comp. Laws Ann. § 340.921, Miss. Code Ann. § 6486-01, Mont. Rev. Codes § 75-6312, Neb. Rev. Stat. § 79-4,125, N.J. Stat. Ann. § 18A:42-5, Ore. Rev. Stat. § 336.610, R.I. Gen. Laws § 16-38-4, Texas Educ. Code § 4.20.

In some states the common law right to regulate fraternities is enacted into statute, and school boards *may* prohibit them: Colo. Rev. Stat. § 123-21-18, La. Rev. Stat. Ann. § 17:2092, Minn. Stat. Ann. § 127.17, Mo. Stat. Ann. § 171.141, N.Y. Educ. Law § 1709-a, 70 Okla. Stat. Ann. § 20-2, 16 Vt. Stat. Ann. § 1164, Wash. Rev. Code Ann. § 26.62.180.

Parents must submit to the authority of the school (quote): *Board of Education* v. *Purse,* page 901.

May punish pupil where parent has refused to abide by a reasonable rule: *Bourne* (sign report card), *Casey County Board of Education* (keep child on school grounds during lunchtime), *Flory* (same), *Stromberg* (remove noisy and destructive heel cleats).

May punish pupil whose parent allows him to be tardy: *Burdick.* 1929–30 Mich. Att. Gen. 412. Cf., *Jackson v. Ellington* (permissible for state to enact statute making it a misdemeanor to induce a pupil to absent himself from school in order to attend a protest).

May punish a pupil whose parent insults a teacher: *Board of Education* v. *Purse.*

In some states it is a criminal misdemeanor to insult a teacher: Ark. Stat. Ann. § 80-1905, Cal. Educ. Code § 13559, Fla. Stat. Ann. § 231.07, Idaho Code § 18-911, Ind. Stat. Ann. § 28-6119, Ky. Rev. Stat. Ann. § 161.190, Miss. Code Ann. § 6216-05, Mont. Rev. Codes § 75-6110, 70 Okla. Stat. Ann. § 6-14, Wash. Rev. Code Ann. § 28.87.010.

In some states it is a criminal misdemeanor to disrupt the school: Cal. Educ. Code § 13558.5, 77 Md. Code Ann. § 96, Mont. Rev.

Codes § 75-8306, Nev. Rev. Stat. § 392.480, N.H. Rev. Stat. Ann. §§ 193:11, 193:15, N.C. Gen. Stat. §§ 14-273, -274, S.C. Code § 16-551, S.D. Comp. Laws § 13-32-6, Tenn. Code Ann. § 39-1214, Tex. 1971 Sess. Laws, Ch. 258, Va. Code § 18.1-240, Wash. Rev. Code Ann. § 28.87.060.

May regulate access to pupils by outside persons; including requiring school personnel to be present: 1961–62 Mich. Att. Gen. 155 (No. 3537).

Warrant takes precedence over school rule: 1959 Fla. Att. Gen. 059-227 (Nov. 13, 1959), 1961–62 Mich. Att. Gen. 155 (No. 3537).

Pupil must prove abuse of discretion: *Board of Education* v. *Booth, State ex rel. Baker, Tanton.*

May assign to grade level: *Pittman.*

May classify by learning ability: *Moore* v. *Tangipahoa Parish School Board, Pittman, Swan,* 52 Ala. Code § 1(8), Ariz. Rev. Stat. § 15-442, N.C. Code § 15-38-14.

. . . unless the classification is based upon racial discrimination: *Moore* v. *Tangipahoa Parish School Board.*

Parent not normally liable for torts of child: 1965 Ky. Att. Gen. 12.

Child is liable for his own torts: *Garratt.*

By statute in some states the parents must pay for a child's malicious damage to property: Alaska Stat. § 34.50.20 (up to $500), Ariz. Rev. Stat. § 15-446, Mich. Comp. Laws Ann. § 600.2913 (up to $1,500), Mont. Rev. Codes § 75-6310, N.J. Stat. Ann. § 18A:37-3 (ruled constitutional in *Board of Education* v. *Hansen*), Okla. 1971 Sess. Laws, Ch. 62 (up to $1,500), Ore. Rev. Stat. § 339.260, S.D. Comp. Laws § 13-32-5, Va. Code § 8-654.1, Wash. Rev. Code Ann. § 28.87.120. Cf., Cal. Educ. Code § 10606 (parents to pay for lost damaged school materials), Nev. Rev. Stat. § 393.170 (same).

Limitations Upon the Teacher's Authority

Summer vacations—rules have no effect: *Wilson* v. *Abilene Independent School District.*

Diploma may not be withheld if pupil has earned it: *State ex rel. Roberts,* Wyo. Stat. § 21.1-64.

Discipline not permissible for postgraduation act: 1960 Mich. Att. Gen. 114 (No. 3545).

May not discipline for pretransfer act: *Stephens.*

Parent is supreme in home (quote): *Hobbs,* page 517.

May not demand that homework be done at specific times: *Hobbs.*

May not ban private parties: *Dritt.*

May not require an activity which violates a pupil's religious beliefs: *Banks* (salute and pledge to the flag), *Hardwick* (dancing), *Mitchell* v. *McCall* (wearing of gym uniform and doing of exercises felt to be immodest), *State* v. *Smith* (salute and pledge to the flag).

Parent may choose courses: *Hardwick, Morrow, School Board* v. *Thompson, State ex rel. Andrews, State ex rel. Sheibley, Trustees of Schools.*

. . . but child's placement may not disrupt the education of others: *Trustees of Schools.*

May not require upkeep of school: *State ex rel. Bowe.*

May not fine pupils: *State ex rel. Dresser.*

May not demand fees from pupils: *Williams* v. *Smith.*

May not create a monopoly: *Hailey.*

May not protect professional musicians: *Gentry.* New Jersey is the only state which has such a statute. N.J. Stat. Ann. § 18A:42-2.

May not punish a pupil who is too poor to pay for intentional property damage: *Allen.*

Ceremony attendance is not a prerequisite for graduation: 1961–62 Ore. Att. Gen. 428. Cf., *State ex rel. Roberts.*

Pupil may not be punished for accidental damage to property: *Holman, Perkins, State* v. *Vanderbilt.*

Pupil may not be punished for acts of other pupils: *State* v. *Thornton.*

Pupil may not be expelled for being married: *Board of Education* v. *Bentley, Carrollton-Farmers Branch Independent School District,* 1925–26 Iowa Att. Gen. 447.

Pupil may not be excluded merely for being an unwed mother: *Nutt, Ordway, Perry.*

Cases involving grooming rules: *Alexander, Bannister, Bishop, Black, Boyle, Breen, Brick, Bright, Brownlee, Calbillo, Carter, Cordova, Corley, Crews, Crossen, Davis* v. *Firment, Dunham, Farrell* v. *Smith, Ferrell, Gfell, Giangreco, Griffin, Jackson* v. *Dorrier, Jeffers, Komadina, Laine, Livingston, Lovelace, Meyers* v. *Arcata Union High School District, Miller* v. *Gillis, Neuhaus, Olff, Pritchard, Reichenberg, Richards, Schwartz, Scott* v. *Board of Education, Shows, Sims, Southern, Stevenson, Westley, Whitsell, Wood, Yoo, Zachry.*

Private schools are not bound by the same restrictions as are public schools: *Bright.*

Some courts put a heavy burden of proof on the school: e.g., *Meyers* v. *Arcata Union High School District.*

Some courts have ruled that choice of grooming is protected by the 14th Amendment: e.g., *Brick, Calbillo, Richards, Sims.*

Some courts have refused to recognize constitutional issues: e.g., *Griffin, Pritchard, Schwartz, Stevenson, Wood.*

One court refused to rule, saying that the issue is up to the legislature: *Alexander.*

Some courts allow pupils to sue as a violation of civil rights: e.g., *Crossen, Westley.*

Some courts demand proof of actual substantial disruptions: e.g., *Breen* (disruptions must be "aggravated . . . frequent . . . general . . . persistent"), *Calbillo, Cordova, Crews, Komadina, Laine, Miller* v. *Gillis, Westley, Yoo, Zachry.*

Some courts require proof of health hazards: e.g., *Bannister, Crews, Komadina, Olff, Scott* v. *Board of Education, Westley.*

Some courts require an explicit written code: e.g., *Crossen* (requiring students to be "neatly dressed and groomed" in "modesty and good taste" and not in "extreme style and fashion" is unconstitutionally vague), *Meyers* v. *Arcata Union High School District* ("extremes of hair style are not acceptable" is unconstitutionally vague).

Some courts look to the reasonableness of classification: e.g., *Griffin* (unreasonable to single out "blocked"—i.e., not tapered—hair as prohibited).

Some courts demand statistical data from the school: *Reichenberg.*

Some courts—may not base regulations upon aesthetics: e.g., *Richards, Zachry.*

Some courts have ruled that conformity is not a permissible goal to pursue: e.g., *Black, Breen, Richards.*

Some courts refuse to require a pupil to cut his hair because of attacks upon him by others: e.g., *Crews, Reichenberg, Westley.*

Some courts have refused to enforce health and safety rules which only apply to male students: e.g., *Crews, Miller* v. *Gillis* (court noted absence of hair regulations for teachers and rhetorically asked why long hair was claimed to be disruptive when worn by male students but acceptable when worn by male teachers).

Some courts have accepted the principal's opinion that there might be distractions: e.g., *Brownlee, Livingston, Schwartz, Shows, Southern, Stevenson, Wood.*

Some courts have accepted testimony that long hair ruins a school's image: e.g., *Brownlee, Farrell* v. *Smith.*

Some courts have ruled that long hair causes low grades: e.g., *Bishop, Brownlee, Jackson* v. *Dorrier, Pritchard, Whitsell.*

Some courts feel that it is permissible for the school to regulate aesthetics: *Brownlee, Carter, Lovelace.*

Some courts feel that they are preventing "unrestrained anarchy": *Livingston, Lovelace.*

One court felt it was protecting the feelings of less mature pupils: *Lovelace.*

One court enforced hair regulations as a method of telling the boys from the girls: *Livingston.*

Some courts have faulted long-haired pupils for being picked upon: *Ferrell, Jeffers, Giangreco, Southern.*

One decision—coach may regulate hair length: *Neuhaus.*

One decision—band instructor may regulate hair length: *Corley.*

One decision—coach may not regulate hair length (quote): *Dunham,* page 420.

Reasoning of decisions is in disarray (quote): *Jeffers,* page 370.

Decisions regarding the teacher's grooming: Two courts have ruled that a public school teacher's wearing of a beard is constitutionally protected, and so he may not be disciplined or fired for wearing one. *Braxton, Finot.*

There is a constitutional right to freedom of speech: *Barker, Tinker.* Neither do teachers give up their rights to freedom of speech. *Abel, Friedman, Ross,* Alaska Stat. § 34.50.20. Cf., *Pickering.*

Rights extend to underground newspapers and political literature: *Dickey, Eisner, Riseman, Scoville, Sullivan.* Cf., *Zucker* (where school newspaper carried pro-Vietnam war articles, other pupils had a right to put in an antiwar ad). Neither may teachers be prohibited from distributing literature on the school grounds. *Friedman.*

Underground newspapers permitted (quote): *Sullivan,* page 1340.

Education is defined broadly: *Tinker.*

Permissible to criticize school personnel: *Scoville, Sullivan.*

Permissible to criticize political figures: *Dickey.*

May not restrict speech because others may overreact: *Sullivan.*

Acts which communicate a point of view are "speech": *Aguirre* (wearing armband), *Banks v. Board of Public Instruction* (refusal to join in Pledge of Allegiance), *Burnside* (wearing a button), *Butts* (wearing armband), *Frain* (refusal to join in Pledge of Allegiance), *Saunders* (joining a peaceful demonstration), *Sheldon* (refusal to stand during National Anthem), *Tinker* (wearing armband). The pupil is similarly protected if his act or refusal is based upon religious teachings. *Banks v. Board of Public Instruction, West Virginia Board of Education.*

Student may not be punished for engaging in a protected activity: *Frain*.

May not prohibit leafletting in public areas: *City of Elizabeth, Mandel*.

Speech may be limited if it materially and substantially interferes with discipline (quote): *Burnside*, page 749; *Dickey*, page 618. See also *Hernandez, Sullivan*.

Speech which materially disrupts the classroom is not protected (quote): *Tinker*, page 513.

A boycott is not a protected activity: *Cavanagh, Hobson*.

A sit-in is not a protected activity: *Farrell* v. *Joel, Kleinjans, Zanders*.

Disruption of a sporting event is not a protected activity: *Barker*.

Violent protest is not permissible: *Esteban*. Cf., *Siegel*. In many states it is a criminal misdemeanor for someone to disrupt the operation of a school.

Wearing of buttons may be prohibited if unusual commotion is created (quote): *Blackwell*, page 754. Also see *Hernandez*.

Wearing of symbol may be prohibited if it becomes an excuse for disruption: *Hernandez* (berets).

Incitement to disruption is not permissible speech: *Siegel*.

Greater restrictions permissible on public school grounds than are allowed on college campuses: *Katz*.

May punish for absences due to protest activities: *Hobson*.

May not prohibit an activity which causes only temporary, mild distraction: *Burnside, Tinker*.

There must be a reasonable fear of substantial disruption in order to prohibit the activity: *Channing Club, Scoville, Tinker*.

The feared danger must be immediate in order to prohibit the activity: *Norton*.

There must be no other practical alternatives to regulation: *Butts*.

In order to prohibit the activity the pupil must be succeeding in his attempt to cause disruption: *Scoville*.

It is not enough to act out of an unspecific fear that something might happen: *Butts, Scoville, Tinker*.

Mere distribution of an underground newspaper or political literature is not a threat to the school: *Channing Club, Eisner, Riseman, Scoville, Sullivan*.

May not require prior approval before distribution on the grounds by students: *Eisner* (underground newspaper), *Riseman* (political literature).

. . . but may do so for material distributed on the grounds by non-students: *State* v. *Oyen*.

Literature urging immediate disruption of school may be suppressed: *Norton* ("stand up and fight").

May prohibit the solicitation of funds on school grounds: *Katz.*
Blanket prohibition on picketing is unconstitutional: *Mosley.*
California Court of Appeals decision—statute barring disruption of schools is unconstitutional: *Castro.*
Statutes prohibiting disruption of schools are constitutional: *City of Rockford, McAlpine, State* v. *Besson, State* v. *Young.* Cf., *Whitfield* (statute providing for suspension for "gross disobedience or misconduct" is constitutional).
Obscenity is not "free speech": *Baker* v. *Downey City Board of Education, Vought.*
Obscenity regulations for juveniles may be more rigorous: *Keefe.*
Vulgar words may be properly included in serious academic discussion: *Keefe, Mailloux.*
May not prohibit publications with words which are accepted in library books: *Keefe, Vought.*
May not ban college newspaper where similar words are in other periodicals sold on campus: *Channing Club.*

Search of Desk or Locker

Constitutional prohibition against "unreasonable searches" does not apply to teachers: *Mercer, Overton, Ranninger.*
. . . or to school officers: *In re Donaldson, Keene, People* v. *Jackson.*
. . . or to private citizens: *Barnes, Burdeau.*
Landlord may not cause tenant's premises to be searched: *Chapman, Niro.*
Hotel may not open a guest's room to the police: *Stoner.*
Employer may not authorize police search of an employee's desk: *United States* v. *Blok.*
Hotel maids may not open a guest's room to the police: *State* v. *Purvis, Stoner.*
Coin locker company may not open lockers for police: *United States* v. *Small.*
May not search locked containers: *Holzhey.*
May make casual inspection of lost article: *Barnes.*
Parent may authorize search of child's room: *State* v. *Carder, State* v. *Haggard.*
Parent may authorize search of child's belongings: *State* v. *Carder.*
School may inspect pupil's desk or locker: *In re Donaldson, People* v. *Overton* (companion case: *Overton*), *State* v. *Stein.* Cf., *Keene* (search of pupil's auto at military college), *Moore* v. *Student Affairs Committee* (search of college dorm room), *People* v. *Jackson* (search of pupil), *People* v. *Tidwell* (search of jail

guard's locker), *Ranninger* (requirement that pupil empty his pockets).

Desk and locker use is not exclusive in relation to the school: *People v. Overton, State v. Stein.* Cf., *People v. Tidwell.*

School authorities have duty to inspect (quote): *People v. Overton,* page 598. See also, *People v. Jackson.*

May not search for personal reasons or purposes: *Phillips.*

Must have "reasonable belief" in order to justify a search: *Moore v. Student Affairs Committee, People v. Jackson.*

Need "probable cause" to call the police: *Boykin, People v. Cohen.*

School must give way to a police warrant: 1961–62 Mich. Att. Gen. 155 (No. 3537).

May not permanently confiscate a nuisance item: cf., *Thoma.*

Suspension and Expulsion

Pupil may be removed from the classroom: *Peck* (physical force permissible).

Detention is permissible: 1961 Ky. Att. Gen. 293.

Activities may be limited: *Kissick.*

Credits and/or diploma may be withheld: 1960 Mich. Att. Gen. 114 (No. 3545). Cf., *Steele.*

Teacher has common law right to suspend a pupil: *Banks v. Seattle School District, Sewell, State ex rel. Burpee.* Cf., *Holman, Rulison.*

Teacher may set reasonable conditions for return to class: *Byrd* (apology in front of classmates).

A factor in considering the propriety of suspension is the seriousness of denying education to a child: *Holman, Nutt, Perkins, Rulison.*

The purpose of suspension is the maintenance of stability in the classroom: *Nutt, Rulison, R.R.*

Basis must be gross or persistent conduct: *Holman, Perkins, Rulison.* Ruled constitutional in *Whitfield.*

Basis may not be a petty or trivial offense (quote): *Holman,* page 997. Also see *Williams v. Smith.*

May not be because the personality or activities of the pupil are distasteful to school authorities: *Scoville, Woody.*

Marriage is not grounds for expulsion: *Board of Education v. Bentley, Carrollton-Farmers Branch Independent School District,* 1925–26 Iowa Att. Gen. 477.

Being an unwed mother is not in itself grounds for expulsion: *Nutt, Ordway, Perry,* Fla. 1971 Session Laws § 21.

Mere failure of subjects is not sufficient grounds for expulsion: 1930 Iowa Att. Gen. 74.

May not be punished for mere carelessness: *Holman.* Cf., *State* v. *Vanderbilt.*

May not suspend pupil merely because he is too poor to pay for damage: *Allen.*

Suspension powers may be exercised only by the official named in the statute or school board rules: *Burnkrant.*

Suspension may last the school year in absence of guidelines: *Board of Education* v. *Purse.*

. . . but may not last more than the school year: *Board of Education* v. *Helston.*

No hearing necessary: e.g., *Davis* v. *Ann Arbor Public Schools, People ex rel. Bluett, Robinson, Vermillion.*

Hearing necessary: e.g., *Banks* v. *Board of Public Instruction, Black Students, Cornette, Dixon, Jones* v. *State Board, Scoggin, Woody.* Cf., *Schiff.* Public school teachers have a due process right to a fair hearing before being dismissed. *Lucia.*

New York decision—right to hearing for any serious punishment: *Goldwyn* (the exam is a prerequisite to attending college in New York).

Less extensive formalities necessary for lesser punishments: *Farrell* v. *Joel, Hasson.* Cf., *Sill* (college).

Recent case—must provide some informal procedure for lesser punishments: *O'Connor.*

Use of Corporal Punishment to Enforce Rules

Corporal punishment not permitted in New Jersey: N.J. Stat. Ann. § 18A:6-1.

States where corporal punishment has been upheld by courts: Alabama (*Suits*); Arkansas (*Berry*); Connecticut (*Sheehan*); Illinois (*Swigert*); Indiana (*Cooper*); Iowa (*Tinkham*); Kentucky (*Carr, Hardy*); Louisiana (*Frank*); Maine (*Stevens*); Missouri (*Haycraft*); Nebraska (*Clasen*); New Hampshire (*Kidder*); North Carolina (Cf., *Drum*); Ohio (*Quinn*); Tennessee (*Marlar*); Texas (*Prendergast*—also ruling that absent a statute a superintendent has no power to utilize corporal punishment since it is not his function to personally control pupils); Vermont (*Lander, Melen*); Wisconsin (*Morrow*).

States where corporal punishment is expressly authorized by statute: Ga. Stat. Ann. §§ 32-835, -836, -837, Hawaii Stat. Ann. § 298-16, Mich. Comp. Laws Ann. §§ 340.756, 340.757, Minn. Stat. Ann. § 609.06, Mont. Rev. Codes § 75-2407, Nev. Rev. Stat. § 392.465, N.Y. Penal Law § 35.10, 24 Pa. Stat. Ann. (interpreted in *Harris, Rupp*), S.D. Comp. Laws § 13-32-2, 16 Vt.

Stat. Ann. § 1161, Va. Code § 22-231.1, Wash. Rev. Code Ann.
§§ 9.11.040, 28.87.140, Wyo. Stat. § 21.1-64 ("reasonable
forms of punishment").

CHAPTER EIGHT: ASSAULT AND BATTERY PROBLEMS

The Law of Assault and Battery

Definition of assault and battery (quote): *Tinkler,* page 203.

Liable for rude touching: *Wilson* v. *Orr* (search inside box in plaintiff's hand).

Liable for potentially injurious touching: *Markley* (roughhouse), *Talmage* (playfully throwing sticks).

Liable for violent touching: *Gungrich* (ejection from house), *Welch* v. *Ware* (physical attack).

Not liable for aiding someone: *Noble* (helping a sick child to stand), *State* v. *Hemphill* (trying to lead a girl away from two strange men).

Not liable for reasonable and customary contact: *Hindy* (touch in a conciliatory manner).

Liable if intended to offensively touch someone: *Talmage.*

Liable if an object is used: *Cornell* (stone), *Talmage* (stick).

Liable for pushing someone down: *Markley.*

Liable even if there is no physical injury: *McFadden, Welch* v. *Ware.*

Must compensate for indignity: *Gungrich, Welch* v. *Ware.*

Jury may award punitive damages: *McFadden, Welch* v. *Ware.*

Provocation may result in mitigation of damages: *Gungrich, Welch* v. *Ware.*

Consent to mutual combat: *Tinkler.*

Consent to a dangerous game: *Markley.* This is the rule which bars assault and battery suits stemming from normal football or boxing activity.

Words never justify an attack: *Gungrich.* However, verbal provocation may lessen the damages.

An uncontrollable temper is no defense: *Welch* v. *Ware.*

Intoxication is no defense: *Welch* v. *Ware.*

Corporal Punishment and Assault and Battery

Must be based upon a reasonable regulation: e.g., *Barry* (unreasonable rule), *Hardy* (trivial difference of opinion), *Melen* (inability to solve a math problem).

Must be reasonable force in light of the offense: e.g., *Carr, Cooper, Johnson.*

Must be reasonable force in light of the pupil's age and physical characteristics: e.g., *Frank, Johnson, Melen, Suits.*

Must be without malice: e.g., *Haycraft, Suits.*

May not use fists: *Wilson v. State.*

Infliction of serious injury does not always result in liability: *Drum* (accident), *Ely* (unknown physical weakness), *Quinn* (same).

Serious injury makes it difficult to show that force used was reasonable: e.g., *Harris, Melen, Rupp.*

Delaware standard for punishment: Del. Stat. § 14-701.

Illinois standard for punishment: 122 Ill. Stat. Ann. § 34-84a.

Oklahoma standard for punishment: 70 Okla. Stat. Ann. § 6-15.

Michigan standard for punishment: Mich. Comp. Laws Ann. §§ 340.756, -.757.

In Delaware, Illinois, Michigan, and Oklahoma the pupil must prove greater abuse, in the form of permanent injury: *State v. Lutz, State v. Thornton.* Cf., *People v. Green.*

. . . or malice: *Fabian, People v. Green, State v. Lutz, State v. Thornton.*

. . . or wanton force: *Ibid.*

Being asked to be strict is no defense: *State v. Thornton.*

Good effect of excessive punishment is no defense: *Ibid.*

May be subject to criminal charges: e.g., *State v. Lutz, State v. Thornton.*

Self-Defense and Defense of Others

May use force reasonably necessary to end threat: *Anders, Hetrick, Thomason.*

Excessive force not permitted: *Anders.*

May not continue force after attacker submits or flees: *Hetrick, Cornell.*

May protect pupils from attack: cf., *Downs* (parental rights to aid offspring) 77 Md. Code Ann. § 98A.

Not liable for mistake: *Ibid.*

Medical Examination and Treatment

Legislature may provide for health care: *McCartney, Wright v. DeWitt School District.*

Absent statutory authority school personnel have no right to provide health care: *Guerrieri,* 1928, Iowa Att. Gen. 150. Cf., *Zoski, Franklyn.* See pages 36–37 for a complete discussion of emergency first aid.

First aid permissible only to prevent serious injury: Cf., *Moss, Tabor.*

The exception is California, where by statute the teacher may apply "reasonable medical treatment" for any injury if the parent cannot be reached. Cal. Educ. Code § 11709.

School may hire nurse to detect pupil sickness: 1943 Mich. Att. Gen. 382 (No. 685).

May not provide health care: 1943 Mich. Att. Gen. 382 (No. 685), 1928 Iowa Att. Gen. 150. In Connecticut, upon written consent by the parent school personnel may administer the child's medicine. Conn. Gen. Stat. Ann. § 10-212a.

May not provide medical treatment: *Guerrieri,* Mich. Comp. Laws Ann. § 340.782, 1943 Mich. Att. Gen. 382 (No. 685).

May not require physical examinations: 1946 Ohio Att. Gen. No. 1340, Mich. Comp. Laws Ann. § 340.782.

Absent emergency, may not take a pupil to the hospital: 1949 Maine Att. Gen. 155. Cf., *Guerrieri.*

Search of Pupil

The average person has no right to search another: *Piggly-Wiggly Alabama Co.*

Within limits, teacher may search a pupil: *Marlar, People* v. *Jackson,* 1964 Ky. Att. Gen. 329. Cf., *Mercer* (principal required pupil to empty pockets).

If search is wrongful, it may be assault and battery: *Phillips.*

Teacher has inherent rights to disarm a pupil: *Christofides, Metcalf.*

In some states statutes expressly state the teachers rights to disarm a pupil: Mich. Comp. Laws Ann. § 340.755, N.J. Stat. Ann. § 18A:6-1. By Mich. Comp. Laws Ann. § 340.757, the Michigan teacher will not be liable for such an action unless he acts with "gross abuse and disregard for the health and safety of the pupil."

CHAPTER NINE: RELEASE OF INFORMATION

Defamation Problems

It is defamation to falsely expose a person to hatred, contempt, or ridicule: *Flynn, Prewitt.*

It is defamation to falsely lower a person's image in the eyes of the community: *Nuyen, Prewitt.*

The purpose of the law of defamation is to protect reputations: *Bonkowski.*

False accusation of mental impairment is defamation: *Everest* ("crazy"), *Kenney* v. *Hatfield.*

False claim of unchastity is defamation: e.g., Mich. Comp. Laws Ann. § 2911.

Defamation to falsely accuse of immoral sexual activity: *Kenney* v. *Gurley, Meyers* v. *Fort.*

False accusation of illegitimacy is defamation: *Harris* v. *Nashville Trust Co.*

Unfounded claim of a loathesome disease is defamation: *Kenney v. Gurley* (venereal disease).

False charge of theft is defamation: *Ellis, Poledna, Zanley.* An accusation of "misappropriation" is the same as that of theft. *Sias.*

Calling a person a liar falsely is defamation: *Prewitt.*

Defamation to call a person a "meddler," etc.: *Von Lonkhuyzen.*

Defamation to call a person a "disturber of the peace," etc.: *Flynn.*

The falsehood need only be communicated to one other person: *Luick.*

No liability for the truth: *Cochrane* v. *Wittbold.* The accusations need not be true in every detail, but need only be substantially similar to the actual facts: *Maguire.*

No liability if the person invited repetition of the charges: *Shingle-meyer.*

Words are read in the "ordinary and popular sense" (quote): *World Publishing Co.,* page 108. See also, *Moore* v. *Booth Pub. Co.*

No liability if the statement is not taken literally: *Ellis, Traynor.*

"Thief" may mean "unfair": *Ellis.*

Less damages if the reputation is already bad: *Georgia.*

Less damages if provoked: *Newman.*

Privileged statement if made in good faith without actual malice (quote): *Zanley,* page 101. Also, *Bostetter.*

Privileged communication may involve a legal duty: *Hansen* (complaint by parent to school superintendent is privileged since the superintendent has the legal responsibility of controlling the school environment).

Privileged communication may involve a moral duty: *Zanley* (accusation of theft communicated to boy's father).

Privileged communication may involve a social duty: *Konkle* (communications about clergy privileged among church members), *Solow* (answer by a former employer to a request for information about a former employee is qualifiedly privileged) Del. Stat. § 14-4114 (qualified privilege for school records).

Communications to the police are privileged: *Wells.*

Communications to public officials are privileged: *Mundy.*

Communications by school personnel to parents are privileged: *Baskett, Everest, Kenney* v. *Gurley.*

Communications by school personnel to the school board are privileged: *Forsythe.*

Communications by school personnel concerning the administration of the schools are privileged: *Pickering.*

Communications *to* school personnel are privileged: *Hansen, Segall* (parent wrote letter to principal about teacher).

Reports to teachers by psychologists are privileged: *Iverson.*

Privilege lost by communication made with ill will: *Poledna.*

Privilege lost by knowing lie: *Froslee.*

Privilege lost if act is not done for the educational welfare of the child: *Jones* v. *Battle.* Cf., *MacLean.*

Abuse of privilege to disclose wrong information to those with no duty to deal with the problem: *Flynn, Poledna, Sias.* In Oklahoma the teacher is also bound by a statute which makes it unlawful for a teacher to reveal information concerning pupils gained in the course of teaching duties, except as it may be required in the performance of those duties. 70 Okla. § 6-16.

School Records

Government records are public: e.g., Mich. Comp. Laws Ann. § 750.492, Neb. Rev. Stat. §§ 84-712, -712.01.

Citizen has access to school board minutes, etc.: 1943–44 Mich. Att. Gen. 2.

Pupil's school file is "quasi-public": cf., *Nowack.*

Parent may not be denied the right to see his child's file: *Van Allen,* Cal. Educ. Code § 10757.

Rule altered by statute in four states: Cal. Educ. Code § 10751, Del. Stat. § 14-4114, Ky. Rev. Stat. Ann. § 164, N.J. Stat. Ann. § 18A:36-19.

Private papers of a teacher are not part of the pupil's "record": cf., 1952–54 Mich. Att. Gen. 306 (private notes of prosecuting attorney are not public records).

Teacher's notes may be "privileged communications": See following section. Cf., *Massachusetts Mutual Life Insurance Co.* (privileged communications between a doctor and patient may not be released for evidence in a law suit).

In the Courtroom

Michigan statute: Mich. Comp. Laws Ann. § 600.2165.

Michigan statute does not affect information gained from nonconfidential sources: *Anderson.*

Montana statute: Mont. Rev. Codes § 93-701-4.

Statutory counselor's privilege in North Dakota: N.D. Code § 31-01-06.1.

Appendix C

Cases Cited

Cases Cited

Abel v. Gousha, 313 F.S. 1030 (E.D. Wis. 1970).

Adams v. Kline, 239 A.2d 230 (Del. 1968).

Aguirre v. Tahoka Independent School District, 311 F.S. 664 (N.D. Texas 1970).

Ahern v. Livermore Union High School District, 208 Cal. 770, 284 P. 1105 (1930).

Akin v. Board of Education, 262 Cal. App. 2d 161, 68 Cal. Rptr. 557 (1968).

Alexander v. Thompson, 313 F.S. 1389 (C.D. Cal. 1970).

Allen v. Chacon, 449 S.W. 2d 289 (Tex. Civ. App. 1970).

Anders v. Clover, 198 Mich. 763, 165 N.W. 640 (1917).

Anderson v. Lavelle, 285 Mich. 194, 280 N.W. 729 (1938).

Appeal of School District of the Borough of Old Forge, 43 D. & C. 167 (Pa. 1941).

Arnold v. Hafling, 474 P. 2d 638 (Colo. App. 1970).

Baker v. Alt, 374 Mich. 492, 132 N.W. 2d 614 (1965).

Baker v. Downey City Board of Education, 307 F.S. 517 (C.D. Cal. 1969).

Balding v. State, 23 Tex. Crim. App. 214, 4 S.W. 579 (1887).

Banks v. Board of Public Instruction, 314 F.S. 285 (S.D. Fla. 1970).

Banks v. Seattle School District, 195 Wash. 321, 80 P. 2d 835 (1938).
Bannister v. Paradis, 316 F.S. 185 (D.N.H. 1970).
Bard v. Board of Education, 140 N.Y.S. 2d 850 (1955).
Barker v. Hardway, 283 F.S. 228 (S.D. W. Va. 1968).
Barnes v. United States, 373 F.2d 517 (5th Cir. 1967).
Baskett v. Crossfield, 190 Ky. 751, 228 S.W. 673 (1921).
Bauer v. Board of Education, 285 A.D. 1148, 140 N.Y.S. 2d 167 (1955).
Beauchamp v. Saginaw Mining Co., 50 Mich. 163, 15 N.W. 65 (1883).
Beck v. San Francisco Unified School District, 225 Cal. App. 2d 503, 37 Cal. Rptr. 471 (1964).
Bellman v. San Francisco High School District, 11 Cal. 2d 576, 81 P.2d 894 (1938).
Bennett v. Board of Education, 15 A.D. 2d 921, 226 N.Y.S. 2d 593 (1962).
Berner v. Board of Education, 286 N.Y. 174, 36 N.E. 2d 100 (1941).
Berry v. Arnold School District, 199 Ark 1118, 137 S.W. 2d 256 (1940).
Bertola v. Board of Education, 1 A.D. 2d 973, 150 N.Y.S. 2d 831 (1956).
Bishop v. Colaw, 316 F.S. 445 (E.D. Mo., E.D. 1970).
Black v. Cothren, 316 F.S. 468 (D. Neb. 1970).
Black Students v. Williams, 317 F.S. 1211 (M.D. Fla. 1970).
Blackwell v. Issaquena County Board of Education, 363 F.2d 749 (5th Cir. 1966).
Board of Directors v. Green, 259 Iowa 1260, 147 N.W. 2d 854 (1967).
Board of Education v. Bentley, 383 S.W. 2d 677 (Ky. 1964).
Board of Education v. Booth, 110 Ky. 807, 62 S.W. 872 (1901).
Board of Education v. Hansen, 56 N.J. Super. 567, 153 A. 2d 393 (1959).
Board of Education v. Helston, 32 Ill. App. 300 (1889).
Board of Education v. Purse, 101 Ga. 422, 28 S.E. 896 (1897).
Bogust v. Iverson, 10 Wis. 2d 129, 102 N.W. 2d 228 (1960).
Bonkowski v. Arlan's Department Store, 12 Mich. App. 88, 162 N.W. 2d 347 (1968).
Bostetter v. Kirsch Co., 319 Mich. 547, 30 N.W. 2d 276 (1948).
Boughn v. Los Angeles City School District, 7 Cal. 2d 347, 46 P. 2d 223 (1935).
Bourne v. Board of Trustees, 35 Neb. 1, 52 N.W. 710 (1892).
Boykin v. People, 39 Ill. 2d 617, 237 N.E. 2d 460 (1968).
Boyle v. Scapple, — F.S. — (D.Ore. 1970), 38 Law Week 2614.

Bozeman v. Morrow, 34 S.W. 2d 654 (Tex. Civ. App. 1931).

Bradley v. Board of Education, 247 A.D. 833, 286 N.Y.S. 186 (1936).

Braxton v. Board of Public Instruction, 303 F.S. 958 (M.D. Fla. 1969).

Breen v. Kahl, 419 F. 2d 1034 (7th Cir. 1969).

Brick v. Board of Education, 305 F.S. 1316 (D. Colo. 1969).

Brigham Young University v. Lillywhite, 118 F. 2d 836 (10th Cir. 1941).

Bright v. Isenbarger, 314 F.S. 1382 (N.D. Ind. 1970).

Briscoe v. School District No. 123, 32 Wash. 2d 353, 201 P. 2d 697 (1949).

Brittan v. State, 103 N.Y.S. 485 (1951).

Brooks v. Board of Education, 29 Misc. 2d 19, 205 N.Y.S. 2d 777 (1960), aff'd 12 N.Y. 2d 971, 189 N.E. 2d 497 (1963).

Brown v. Greer, 296 F.S. 595 (S.D. Miss., W.D. 1969).

Brown v. Wells, 288 Minn. 468, 181 N.W. 2d 708 (1970).

Brownlee v. Bradley County, Tennessee, Board of Education, 311 F.S. 1316 (E.D. Tenn., S.D. 1970).

Burdeau v. McDowell, 256 U.S. 465 (1921).

Burdick v. Babcock, 31 Iowa 562 (1871).

Burnkraut v. Saggau, 12 Ariz. App. 310, 470 P.2d 115 (1970).

Burnside v. Byars, 363 F. 2d 744 (5th Cir. 1966).

Butler v. District of Columbia, 417 F. 2d 1150 (D.C. Cir. 1969).

Butrick v. Snyder, 236 Mich. 300, 210 N.W. 311 (1926).

Butts v. Dallas Independent School District, 436 F.2d 728 (5th Cir. 1971).

Buzzard v. East Lake School District, 34 Cal. App. 2d 316, 93 P. 2d 233 (1939).

Byrd v. Begley, 262 Ky. 422, 90 S.W.2d 370 (1936).

Calandri v. Ione Unified School District, 219 Cal. App. 2d 542, 33 Cal. Rptr. 333 (1963).

Calbillo v. San Jacinto Junior College, 305 F.S. 857 (S.D. Texas 1969).

Cambareri v. Board of Education, 246 A.D. 127, 284 N.Y.S. 892 (1936).

Campbell v. Brown, 276 Mich. 449, 267 N.W. 887 (1936).

Carabba v. Anacortes School District, 72 Wash. 2d 939, 435 P. 2d 936 (1967).

Carr v. Wright, 423 S.W. 2d 521 (Ky. 1968).

Carrollton-Farmers Branch Independent School District v. Knight, 418 S.W. 2d 535 (Tex. Civ. App. 1967).

Carter v. Hodges, 317 F.S. 89 (W.D. Ark. 1970).

Casey County Board of Education v. Luster, 282 S.W. 2d 333 (Ky. App. 1955).

Castro v. Superior Court, 9 Cal. App. 3d 675, 88 Cal. Rptr. 500 (1970).

Cavanagh v. Galamison, 31 A.D. 635, 297 N.Y.S. 2d 651 (1968).

Channing Club v. Board of Regents, 317 F.S. 688 (N.D. Tex. 1970).

Chapman v. United States, 365 U.S. 610 (1961).

Charonnat v. San Francisco Unified School District, 56 Cal. App. 2d 840, 133 P. 2d 643 (1943).

Cherney v. Board of Education, 31 A.D. 2d 764, 297 N.Y.S. 2d 668 (1969).

Chimerofsky v. School District, 121 Ill. App. 2d 371, 257 N.E. 2d 480 (1970).

Chmela v. Board of Education, 26 Misc. 2d 10, 207 N.Y.S. 2d 401 (1960).

Christofides v. Hellenic Eastern Orthodox Christian Church of New York, 33 Misc. 2d 741, 227 N.Y.S. 2d 946 (1962).

Cianci v. Board of Education, 18 A.D. 2d 930, 238 N.Y.S. 2d 547 (1963).

Cioffi v. Board of Education, 27 A.D. 2d 826, 278 N.Y.S. 2d 826 (1967).

Cirillo v. City of Milwaukee, 34 Wis. 2d 705, 150 N.W. 2d 460 (1967).

City of Elizabeth v. Sullivan, 100 N.J. Super. 51, 241 A.2d 41 (1968).

City of Rockford v. Grayned, 46 Ill. 2d 486, 263 N.E. 2d 866 (1970).

Clark v. Board of Education, 304 N.Y. 488, 109 N.E. 2d 73 (1952).

Clasen v. Pruhs, 69 Neb. 278, 95 N.W. 640 (1903).

Clemmens v. City of Sault Ste. Marie, 289 Mich. 254, 286 N.W. 232 (1939).

Cochrane v. Board of Education, 360 Mich. 390, 103 N.W. 2d 569 (1960).

Cochrane v. Wittbold, 359 Mich. 402, 102 N.W. 2d 459 (1960).

Coggins v. Board of Education, 223 N.C. 763, 28 S.E. 2d 527 (1944).

Comstock v. General Motors Corp., 358 Mich. 163, 99 N.W. 2d 627 (1959).

Conway v. Board of Education, 11 Misc. 2d 162, 171 N.Y.S. 2d 533 (1958).

Cooper v. McJunkin, 4 Ind. 290 (1853).

Cordova v. Chonko, 315 F.S. 953 (N.D. Ohio, W.D. 1970).

Corley v. Daunhauer, 312 F.S. 811 (E.D. Ark. 1970).

Cornell v. Fidler, 194 Mich. 509, 160 N.W. 840 (1916).

Cornette v. Aldridge, 408 S.W. 2d 935 (Tex. Civ. App. 1966).

Crabbe v. County School Board, 164 S.E. 2d 639 (Va. App. 1968).

Crews v. Cloncs, 432 F.2d 1259 (7th Cir. 1970).

Crossen v. Fatsi, 309 F.S. 114 (D. Conn. 1970).

Dailey v. Los Angeles Unified School District, 87 Cal. Rptr. 376, 470 P.2d 360 (1970).

Damgaard v. Oakland High School District, 212 Cal. 316, 298 P. 983 (1931).

Daniels v. Board of Education, 191 Mich. 339, 158 N.W. 23 (1916).

Davis v. Ann Arbor Public Schools, 313 F.S. 1217 (E.D. Mich., S.D. 1970).

Davis v. Firment, 269 F.S. 524 (E.D. La. 1967).

Davis v. Gavalas, 37 Ga. App. 242, 139 S.E. 577 (1927).

DeBenedittis v. Board of Education, 271 A.D. 886, 67 N.Y.S. 2d 31 (1946).

Decker v. Dundee Central School, 4 N.Y. 2d 462, 151 N.E. 866 (1958).

Deisenrieter v. Kraus-Merkel Malting Co., 92 Wis. 164, 72 N.W. 735 (1897).

DeNoyer v. City of Ann Arbor, 9 Mich. App. 26, 155 N.W. 2d 689 (1967).

Deskins v. Gose, 85 Mo. 485 (1885).

Dickey v. Alabama State Board of Education, 273 F.S. 613 (M.D. Ala. 1967).

Dixon v. Alabama State Board of Education, 294 F. 2d 150 (5th Cir. 1961).

Doktor v. Greenberg, 58 N.J. Super 155, 155 A. 2d 793 (1959).

Domino v. Mercurio, 17 A.D. 2d 342, 234 N.Y.S. 2d 1011 (1962).

Douglas v. Campbell, 89 Ark. 254, 116 S.W. 211 (1909).

Dowlen v. State, 14 Tex. App. 61 (1883).

Downs v. Jackson, 128 S.W. 339 (Ky. App. 1910).

Dritt v. Snodgrass, 66 Mo. 286 (1877).

Drum v. Miller, 135 N.C. 204, 47 S.E. 421 (1904).

Duda v. Gaines, 12 N.J. Super. 326, 79 A.2d 695 (1951).

Duncan v. Koustenis, 260 Md. 98, 271 A.2d 547 (1970).

Dunham v. Pulsifer, 312 F.S. 411 (D. Vt. 1970).

Dutcher v. City of Santa Rosa High School District, 156 Cal. App. 2d 256, 319 P. 2d 14 (1958).

Eastman v. Williams, 124 Vt. 445, 207 A. 2d 146 (1965).

Eisner v. Stamford Board of Education, 314 F.S. 832 (D. Conn. 1970).

Ellis v. Burns Valley School District, 128 Cal. App. 550, 18 P. 2d 79 (1933).

Ellis v. Whitehead, 95 Mich. 105, 54 N.W. 752 (1893).

Ely v. State, 68 Tex. Crim. App. 562, 152 S.W. 631 (1913).

Engel v. Gosper, 71 N.J. Super. 573, 177 A. 2d 595 (1962).

Estay v. LaFourche Parish School Board, 230 So. 2d 443 (La. App. 1969).

Esteban v. Central Missouri State College, 415 F. 2d 1077 (8th Cir. 1969).

Everest v. McKenney, 195 Mich. 649, 162 N.W. 277 (1917).

Fabian v. State, 235 Md. 306, 201 A. 2d 511 (1964).

Farah v. Farah, 99 N.Y.S. 2d 972 (1950).

Farrell v. Joel, 437 F.2d 160 (2nd Cir. 1971).

Farrell v. Smith, 310 F.S. 732 (D. Maine, S.D. 1970).

Fein v. Board of Education, 305 N.Y. 611, 111 N.E. 2d 732 (1953).

Felgner v. Anderson, 375 Mich. 23, 133 N.W. 2d 136 (1965).

Ferraro v. Board of Education, 32 Misc. 2d 563, 212 N.Y.S. 2d 615 (1961).

Ferreira v. Sanchez, 79 N.M. 768, 449 P. 2d 784 (1969).

Ferrell v. Dallas Independent School District, 392 F. 2d 697 (5th Cir. 1968).

Fertich v. Michener, 111 Ind. 472, 11 N.E. 605, 14 N.E. 68 (1887).

Feuerstein v. Board of Education, 202 N.Y.S. 2d 524 (1960), aff'd 13 A.D. 2d 503, 214 N.Y.S. 2d 654 (1961).

Finot v. Pasadena City Board of Education, 250 Cal. App. 2d 189, 58 Cal. Rptr. 520 (1967).

Fitzpatrick v. Board of Central School District, 54 Misc. 2d 1085, 284 N.Y.S. 2d 590 (1967).

Flory v. Smith, 145 Va. 164, 134 S.E. 360 (1926).

Flynn v. Boglarsky, 164 Mich. 513, 129 N.W. 674 (1911).

Ford v. Riverside School District, 121 Cal. App. 2d 554, 263 P. 2d 626 (1953).

Forgnone v. Salvadore Union Elementary School District, 41 Cal. App. 2d 423, 106 P. 2d 932 (1940).

Forsythe v. Durham, 270 N.Y. 141, 200 N.E. 674 (1936).

Fortney v. Stephan, 237 Mich. 603, 213 N.W. 172 (1927).

Frace v. Long Beach City High School District, 58 Cal. App. 2d 566, 137 P. 2d 60 (1943).

Frain v. Baron, 307 F.S. 27 (E.D. N.Y. 1969).

Frank v. Orleans Parish School Board, 195 So. 2d 451 (La. App. 1967).

Franklyn v. Peabody, 249 Mich. 363, 228 N.W. 681 (1930).

Friedman v. Union Free School District, 314 F.S. 223 (E.D. N.Y. 1970).

Froslee v. Lund's State Bank of Vining, 131 Minn. 435, 155 N.W. 619 (1915).

Furtado v. Montebello Unified School District, 206 Cal. App. 2d 72, 23 Cal. Rptr. 476 (1962).

Fustin v. Board of Education, 101 Ill. App. 2d 113, 242 N.E. 2d 308 (1968).

Gaincott v. Davis, 281 Mich. 515, 275 N.W. 229 (1937).

Gallagher v. City of New York, 30 A.D. 688, 292 N.Y.S. 2d 139 (1968).

Garber v. Central School District, 251 A.D. 214, 295 N.Y.S. 850 (1937).

Gardner v. State, 281 N.Y. 212, 22 N.E. 2d 344 (1939).

Garratt v. Dailey, 46 Wash. 2d 197, 279 P. 2d 1091 (1955).

Gattavara v. Lundin, 166 Wash. 548, 7 P. 2d 958 (1932).

Gentry v. Memphis Federation of Musicians, 177 Tenn. 566, 151 S.W. 2d 1081 (1941).

Georgia v. Bond, 114 Mich. 196, 72 N.W. 232 (1897).

Germond v. Board of Education, 10 A.D. 2d 139, 197 N.Y.S. 2d 548 (1960).

Gfell v. Rickelman, 313 F.S. 364 (N.D. Ohio, E.D. 1970).

Giangreco v. Center School District, 313 F.S. 776 (W.D. Mo., W.D. 1969).

Gilbert v. Sacramento Unified School District, 258 Cal. App. 2d 505, 65 Cal. Rptr. 913 (1968).

Goldberg v. Regents of the University of California, 248 Cal. App. 2d 867, 57 Cal. Rptr. 463 (1967).

Goldwyn v. Allen, 54 Misc. 2d 94, 281 N.Y.S. 2d 899 (1967).

Gonzales v. Mackler, 19 A.D. 2d 229, 241 N.Y.S. 2d 254 (1963).

Goodman v. Pasadena City High School District, 4 Cal. App. 2d 65, 40 P. 2d 854 (1935).

Govel v. Board of Education, 267 A.D. 621, 48 N.Y.S. 2d 299 (1944).

Greathouse v. Horowitz, 439 Pa. 62, 264 A.2d 665 (1970).

Gregory v. Board of Education, 225 N.Y.S. 679, 222 A.D. 284 (1927).

Griffin v. Tatum, 425 F. 2d 201 (5th Cir. 1970).

Grosso v. Witteman, 266 Wis. 17, 62 N.W. 2d 386 (1954).

Guerrieri v. Tyson, 147 Pa. Super. 239, 24 A. 2d 468 (1942).

Gungrich v. Anderson, 189 Mich. 144, 155 N.W. 379 (1915).

Guyten v. Rhodes, 65 Ohio App. 163, 29 N.E. 2d 444 (1940).

Guzick v. Drebus, 431 F.2d 594 (6th Cir. 1970).

Hailey v. Brooks, 191 S.W. 781 (Tex. Civ. App. 1916).

Haltom v. Burleson, 9 Mich. App. 89, 148 N.W. 2d 252 (1967).

Hammond v. South Carolina State College, 272 F.S. 947 (D. S.C. 1967).

Hansen v. Hansen, 126 Minn. 426, 148 N.W. 457 (1914).

Hardwick v. Board of School Trustees, 54 Cal. App. 696, 205 P. 49 (1921).

Hardy v. James, 5 Ky. Ops. 36 (1872).

Harris v. Crawley, 170 Mich. 381, 136 N.W. 356 (1912).

Harris v. Nashville Trust Co., 128 Tenn. 573, 162 S.W. 584 (1914).

Hasson v. Boothby, 318 F.S. 1183 (D. Mass. 1970).

Haycraft v. Grigsby, 88 Mo. App. 354 (1901).

Haymes v. Catholic Bishop of Chicago, 41 Ill. 2d 336, 243 N.E. 2d 203 (1968).

Hendrickson v. Hodkin, 276 N.Y. 252, 11 N.E. 2d 899 (1937).

Henry v. Garden Grove Union High School District, 119 Cal. App. 638, 7 P. 2d 192 (1932).

Heritage v. Dodge, 64 N.H. 297, 9 A. 722 (1887).

Hernandez v. School District, 315 F.S. 289 (D. Colo. 1970).

Hetrick v. Crouch, 141 Mich. 649, 105 N.W. 131 (1905).

Hindy v. Avedisian, 339 Mich. 616, 64 N.W. 2d 676 (1954).

Hobbs v. Germany, 94 Miss. 469, 49 So. 515 (1909).

Hobson v. Bailey, 309 F.S. 1393 (W.D. Tenn., W.D. 1970).

Holman v. School Trustees, 77 Mich. 605, 43 N.W. 996 (1889).

Holroyd v. Eibling, 116 Ohio App. 440, 188 N.E. 2d 797 (1962).

Holzhey v. United States, 223 F. 2d 823 (5th Cir. 1955).

Huff v. Compton City Grammar School District, 92 Cal. App. 44, 267 P. 918 (1928).

Hurley v. Eddingfield, 156 Ind. 416, 59 N.E. 1058 (1901).

Hutchins v. School District, 114 Wash. 548, 195 P. 1020 (1921).

Hutchison v. Toews, 476 P.2d 822 (Ore. App. 1970).

Hutton v. State, 23 Tex. Crim. App. 386, 5 S.W. 122 (1887).

Iacona v. Board of Education, 285 A.D. 1168, 140 N.Y.S. 2d 539 (1955).

In re Donaldson, 269 Cal. App. 593, 75 Cal. Rptr. 220 (1969).

Iverson v. Frandsen, 237 F. 2d 898 (10th Cir. 1956).

Jackson v. Dorrier, 424 F. 2d 213 (6th Cir. 1970).

Jackson v. Ellington, 316 F.S. 1071 (W.D. Tenn. 1970).

Jakubiec v. Hasty, 337 Mich. 205, 59 N.W. 2d 385 (1953).

Jarrett v. Goodall, 113 W. Va. 478, 168 S.E. 763 (1933).

Jeffers v. Yuba City Unified School District, 319 F.S. 368 (E.D. Cal. 1970).

Johnson v. Horace Mann Mutual Insurance Co., 241 So. 2d 588 (La. App. 1970).

Jones v. Battle, 315 F.S. 601 (D. Conn. 1970).

Jones v. Cody, 132 Mich. 13, 92 N.W. 495 (1902).

Jones v. Jones, 119 Ga. App. 788, 168 S.E. 2d 883 (1969).

Jones v. State Board of Tennessee, 279 F.S. 190 (M.D. Tenn. 1968).

Kaske v. Board of Education, 77 Ill. App. 2d 311, 222 N.E. 2d 921 (1967).

Katz v. McAulay, 438 F. 2d 1058 (2nd Cir. 1971).

Kaufman v. City of New York, 30 Misc. 2d 285, 214 N.Y.S. 2d 767 (1961).

Keefe v. Geanakos, 418 F. 2d 359 (1st Cir. 1969).

Keesee v. Board of Education, 37 Misc. 2d 414, 235 N.Y.S. 2d 300 (1962).

Kelley v. School District, 102 Wash. 343, 173 P. 333 (1918).

Kenney v. Gurley, 208 Ala. 623, 95 So. 34 (1923).

Kenney v. Hatfield, 351 Mich. 498, 88 N.W. 2d 535 (1958).

Kerby v. Elk Grove Union High School District, 1 Cal. App. 2d 246, 36 P. 2d 431 (1934).

Kerwin v. County of San Mateo, 176 Cal. App. 2d 304, 1 Cal. Rptr. 437 (1960).

Kidder v. Chellis, 59 N.H. 473 (1879).

Kidwell v. School District, 53 Wash. 2d 672, 335 P. 2d 805 (1959).

Kinzer v. Directors of Independent School District, 129 Iowa 441, 105 N.W. 686 (1906).

Kissick v. Garland Independent School District, 330 S.W. 2d 708 (Tex. Civ. App. 1959).

Kleinjans v. Lombardi, — Haw. —, 478 P.2d 320 (1970).

Klenzendorf v. Shasta Union High School District, 4 Cal. App. 2d 164, 40 P. 2d 878 (1935).

Komadina v. Peckham, 478 P.2d 113 (Ariz. App. 1970).

Konkle v. Haven, 140 Mich. 472, 103 N.W. 850 (1905).

Kotarski v. Aetna Casualty and Surety Co., 244 F.S. 547 (E.D. Mich. 1965), aff'd 372 F.2d 95 (6th Cir. 1967).

Laine v. Dittman, 125 Ill. App. 2d 136, 259 N.E. 2d 824 (1970).

Lander v. Seaver, 32 Vt. 114 (1859).

LaValley v. Standford, 272 A.D. 183, 70 N.Y.S. 2d 460 (1947).

Lawes v. Board of Education, 16 N.Y. 2d 302, 213 N.E. 2d 667 (1965).

Lee v. Board of Education, 263 A.D. 23, 31 N.Y.S. 2d 113 (1941).

Lee v. Hoffman, 182 Iowa 1216, 166 N.W. 565 (1918).

Lehmuth v. Longbeach Union School District, 53 Cal. 2d 544, 348 P. 2d 887 (1960).

Leibowitz v. Board of Education, 112 N.Y.S. 2d 698 (1952).

Leonard v. School Committee, 349 Mass. 704, 212 N.E. 2d 468 (1965).

Lilienthal v. San Leandro Unified School District, 139 Cal. App. 2d 453, 293 P. 2d 889 (1956).

Lillibridge v. McCann, 117 Mich. 84, 75 N.W. 288 (1898).

Livingston v. Swanquist, 314 F.S. 1 (N.D. Ill., E.D. 1970).

Lopez v. City of New York, 4 A.D. 2d 48, 163 N.Y.S. 2d 562 (1957).

Lovelace v. Leechburg Area School District, 310 F.S. 579 (W.D. Pa. 1970).

Luce v. Board of Education, 2 A.D. 2d 502, 157 N.Y.S. 2d 123 (1956).

Lucia v. Duggan, 303 F.S. 112 (D. Mass. 1969).

Luick v. Driscoll, 13 Ind. App. 279, 41 N.E. 463 (1895).

MacLean v. Scripps, 52 Mich. 214, 17 N.W. 815 (1883).

Madera v. Board of Education, 386 F. 2d 778 (2nd Cir. 1967).

Maede v. Oakland High School District, 212 Cal. 419, 298 P. 987 (1931).

Maguire v. Vaughan, 106 Mich. 280, 64 N.W. 44 (1895).

Mailloux v. Kiley, 323 F.S. 1387 (D. Mass. 1971).

Mandel v. Municipal Court, 276 Cal. App. 788, 81 Cal. Rptr. 173 (1969).

Marino v. Waters, 220 So. 2d 802 (La. 1969).

Markley v. Whitman, 95 Mich. 236, 54 N.W. 763 (1893).

Marlar v. Bill, 181 Tenn. 100, 178 S.W.2d 634 (1944).

Marques v. Riverside Military Academy, 87 Ga. App. 370, 73 S.E. 2d 574 (1952).

Massachusetts Mutual Life Insurance Co. v. Board of Trustees, 178 Mich. 193, 144 N.W. 538 (1913).

Mastrangelo v. West Side Union High School District, 2 Cal. 2d 540, 42 P. 2d 634 (1935).

McAlpine v. Reese, 309 F.S. 136 (E.D. Mich., S.D. 1970).

McCartney v. Austin, 31 A.D. 2d 370, 298 N.Y.S. 2d 26 (1969).

McClarren v. Buck, 343 Mich. 300, 72 N.W. 2d 31 (1955).

McDonell v. Bozo, 285 Mich. 38, 280 N.W. 100 (1938).

McFadden v. Tate, 350 Mich. 84, 85 N.W. 2d 181 (1957).

McLendon v. Hampton Cotton Mills Co., 109 S.C. 238, 95 S.E. 781 (1917).

McLeod v. Grant County School District, 42 Wash. 2d 316, 255 P. 2d 360 (1953).

Norton v. Discipline Committee, 419 F. 2d 195 (6th Cir. 1969).

Nowack v. Fuller, 243 Mich. 200, 219 N.W. 749 (1928).

Nutt v. Board of Education, 128 Kan. 507, 278 P. 1065 (1929).

Nuyen v. Slater, 372 Mich. 654, 127 N.W. 2d 369 (1964).

O'Connor v. Board of Education, 316 N.Y.S. 2d 799 (1970).

Ogando v. Carquinez Grammar School District, 24 Cal. App. 2d 567, 75 P. 2d 641 (1938).

Ohman v. Board of Education, 300 N.Y. 306, 90 N.E. 2d 474 (1949).

Olff v. East Side Union High School District, 305 F.S. 557 (N.D. Cal. 1969).

Ollet v. Pittsburgh, C.C. & St. Louis Ry., 201 Pa. 361, 50 A. 1010 (1902).

Ordway v. Hargraves, 323 F.S. 1155 (D. Mass. 1971).

O'Rourke v. Walker, 102 Conn. 130, 128 A. 25 (1925).

Osterlind v. Hill, 263 Mass. 73, 160 N.E. 301 (1928).

Ostrowski v. Board of Education, 31 A.D. 2d 571, 294 N.Y.S. 2d 871 (1968).

Overton v. Rieger, 311 F.S. 1035 (S.D.N.Y. 1970).

Parks v. Starks, 342 Mich. 443, 70 N.W. 2d 805 (1955).

Passel v. Fort Worth Independent School District, 453 S.W. 2d 888 (Tex. Civ. App. 1970).

Peck v. Smith, 41 Conn. 442 (1874).

People ex rel. Bluett v. Board of Trustees, 10 Ill. App. 2d 207, 134 N.E. 2d 635 (1956).

People v. Cohen, 57 Misc. 2d 366, 292 N.Y.S. 2d 366 (1968).

People v. Green, 155 Mich. 524, 119 N.W. 1087 (1909).

People v. Jackson, 319 N.Y.S. 2d 731 (1971).

People v. Overton, 20 N.Y. 2d 360, 229 N.E. 2d 596 (1967).

People v. Tidwell, — Ill. App. 2d —, 266 N.E. 2d 787 (1971).

Perkins v. Board of Directors, 56 Iowa 476, 9 N.W. 356 (1880).

Perry v. Genada Municipal Separate School District, 300 F.S. 748 (N.D. Miss., W.D. 1969).

Phillips v. Johns, 12 Tenn. App. 354 (1930).

Pickering v. Board of Education, 391 U.S. 563 (1968).

Piggly-Wiggly Alabama Co. v. Rickles, 212 Ala. 585, 103 So. 860 (1925).

Pirkle v. Oakdale Union Grammar School District, 40 Cal. 2d 207, 253 P. 2d 1 (1953).

Pittman v. Board of Education, 56 Misc. 2d 51, 287 N.Y.S. 2d 551 (1967).

Poledna v. Bendix Aviation Corp., 360 Mich. 129, 103 N.W. 2d 789 (1960).

Pollard v. Board of Education, 280 A.D. 1033, 117 N.Y.S. 2d 184 (1952).

Prewitt v. Wilson (128 Iowa 198, 103 N.W. 365 (1903).

Pritchard v. Spring Branch Independent School District, 308 F.S. 570 (S.D. Tex. 1970).

Purcell v. St. Paul City R. Co., 48 Minn. 134, 50 N.W. 1034 (1892).

Queen Insurance Co. v. Hammond, 374 Mich. 655, 132 N.W. 2d 792 (1965).

Quigley v. School District, 251 Ore. 452, 446 P. 2d 177 (1968).

Quinn v. Nolan, 7 Ohio Dec. Reprint 585 (1879).

Ragonese v. Hilferty, 231 Md. 520, 191 A. 2d 422 (1963).

Ranninger v. State, 460 S.W. 2d 182 (Tex. Civ. App. 1970).

Raymond v. Paradise Unified School District, 28 Cal. App. 2d 1, 31 Cal. Rptr. 847 (1963).

Reagh v. San Francisco Unified School District, 119 Cal. App. 2d 65, 259 P. 2d 43 (1953).

Reichenberg v. Nelson, 310 F.S. 248 (D. Neb. 1970).

Reithardt v. Board of Education, 43 Cal. App. 2d 629, 111 P. 2d 440 (1941).

Reynolds v. State, 207 Misc. 963, 141 N.Y.S. 2d 615 (1955).

Richards v. Thurston, 424 F. 2d 1281 (1st Cir. 1970).

Richardson v. Braham, 125 Neb. 142, 249 N.W. 557 (1933).

Ridge v. Boulder Creek Union Junior–Senior High School District, 60 Cal. App. 2d 453, 140 P. 2d 990 (1943).

Riseman v. School Committee, 439 F. 2d 148 (1st Cir. 1971).

Robinson v. University of Miami, 100 So. 2d 442 (Fla. App. 1958).

Rodrigues v. San Jose Unified School District, 157 Cal. App. 2d 842, 322 P. 2d 70 (1958).

Rodriguez v. Brunswick Corp., 364 F. 2d 282 (3rd Cir. 1966).

Rook v. State, 254 A.D. 67, 4 N.Y.S. 2d 116 (1938).

Rose v. Board of Education, 184 Kan. 486, 337 P. 2d 652 (1959).

Ross v. San Francisco Unified School District, 120 Cal. App. 2d 185, 260 P. 2d 663 (1953).

Roth v. Board of Regents, 310 F.S. 972 (W.D. Wis. 1970).

Rounds v. Phillips, 166 Md. 151, 170 A. 532 (1934).

R.R. v. Board of Education, 109 N.J. Super. 337, 236 A. 2d 180 (1970).

Rulison v. Post, 79 Ill. 567 (1875).

Rupp v. Zintner, 29 Pa. D. & C. 625 (1937).

Samuel Benedict Memorial School v. Bradford, 111 Ga. 801, 36 S.E. 920 (1900).

Sanchick v. Board of Education, 11 Misc. 2d 876, 172 N.Y.S. 2d 748 (1958).

Sanders v. Louisiana High School Athletic Association, 242 So. 2d 19 (La. App. 1970).

Satarino v. Sleight, 54 Cal. App. 2d 278, 129 P. 2d 35 (1942).

Saunders v. Virginia Polytechnic Institute, 417 F. 2d 1127 (4th Cir. 1969).

Sayers v. Ranger, 16 N.J. Super. 22, 83 A. 2d 775 (1951).

Sayers v. School District, 366 Mich. 217, 114 N.W. 2d 191 (1962).

Schiff v. Hannah, 282 F.S. 381 (W.D. Mich., S.D. 1966).

School Board v. Thompson, 24 Okla. 1, 103 P. 578 (1909).

Schuyler v. Board of Education, 18 A.D. 2d 406, 239 N.Y.S. 2d 769 (1963).

Schwartz v. Galveston Independent School District, 309 F.S. 1034 (S.D. Tex. 1970).

Schwartz v. Schuker, 298 F.S. 238 (E.D. N.Y. 1969).

Scoggin v. Lincoln University, 291 F.S. 161 (W.D. Mo. 1968).

Scott v. Board of Education, 61 Misc. 2d 333, 305 N.Y.S. 2d 601 (1969).

Scott v. Kilpatrick, 286 Ala. 129, 237 So. 2d 652 (1970).

Scoville v. Board of Education, 425 F. 2d 10 (7th Cir. 1970).

Segall v. Piazza, 46 Misc. 2d 700, 260 N.Y.S. 2d 543 (1965).

Segerman v. Jones, 256 Md. 109, 259 A. 2d 794 (1969).

Selleck v. Board of Education, 276 A.D. 263, 94 N.Y.S. 2d 318 (1949).

Sewell v. Board of Education, 29 Ohio St. 89 (1876).

Sheldon v. Fannin, 221 F.S. 766 (D. Ariz. 1963).

Sheehan v. Sturges, 53 Conn. 481, 2 A. 841 (1885).

Shinglemeyer v. Wright, 124 Mich. 230, 82 N.W. 887 (1900).

Shows v. Freeman, 230 So. 2d 63 (Miss. 1969).

Sias v. General Motors Corp., 372 Mich. 542, 127 N.W. 2d 357 (1964).

Siegel v. Regents of the University of California, 308 F.S. 832 (N.D. Cal. 1970).

Sill v. Pennsylvania State University, 318 F.S. 608 (M.D. Pa. 1970).

Silverman v. City of New York, 28 Misc. 2d 20, 211 N.Y.S. 2d 560 (1961).

Sims v. Colfax Community School District, 307 F.S. 485 (S.D. Iowa, C.D. 1970).

Solow v. General Motors Truck Co., 64 F. 2d 105 (2nd Cir. 1933).

Southern v. Board of Trustees, 318 F.S. 355 (N.D. Tex. 1970).

Stahl v. Southern Michigan Ry. Co., 211 Mich. 350, 178 N.W. 710 (1920).

Stanley v. Gary, 237 S.C. 237, 116 S.E. 2d 843 (1960).

State ex rel. Andrews v. Webber, 108 Ind. 31, 8 N.E. 708 (1886).

State ex rel. Baker v. Stephenson, 94 Ohio L. Abs. 545, 189 N.E. 2d 181 (C. Pl. 1962).

State ex rel. Bowe v. Board of Education, 63 Wis. 234, 23 N.W. 102 (1885).

State ex rel. Burpee v. Burton, 45 Wis. 150 (1878).

State ex rel. Dresser v. District Board, 135 Wis. 619, 116 N.W. 232 (1908).

State ex rel. Evans v. Fry, 11 Ohio Misc. 231, 230 N.E. 2d 363 (C. Pl. 1967).

State ex rel. Indiana High School Athletic Association v. Lawrence Circuit Court, 240 Ind. 114, 162 N.E. 2d 250 (1959).

State ex rel. Roberts v. Wilson, 221 Mo. App. 9, 297 S.W. 419 (1927).

State ex rel. Sheibley v. School District, 31 Neb. 552, 48 N.W. 393 (1891).

State v. Besson, 110 N.J. Super. 528, 266 A. 2d 175 (1970).

State v. Carder, 9 Ohio St. 2d 1, 222 N.E. 2d 620 (1966).

State v. Haggard, 89 Idaho 217, 404 P. 2d 580 (1965).

State v. Hemphill, 162 N.C. 632, 78 S.E. 167 (1913).

State v. Lutz, 65 Ohio L. Abs. 402, 113 N.E. 2d 757 (1953).

State v. Oyen, 78 Wash. 2d 934 480 P.2d 766 (1971).

State v. Purvis, 249 Ore. 404, 438 P. 2d 1002 (1968).

State v. Smith, 155 Kan. 588, 127 P. 2d 518 (1942).

State v. Stein, 203 Kan. 638, 456 P. 2d 1 (1969).

State v. Thornton, 136 N.C. 610, 48 S.E. 602 (1904).

State v. Vanderbilt, 116 Ind. 11, 18 N.E. 266 (1888).

State v. Young, 57 N.J. 240, 271 A. 2d 569 (1970).

Station v. Travelers Insurance Company, 236 So. 2d 610 (La. App. 1970).

Steele v. Sexton, 253 Mich. 32, 234 N.W. 436 (1931).

Stehn v. Bernarr MacFadden Foundations, 434 F. 2d 811 (6th Cir. 1970).

Stephens v. Humphrey, 145 Ark. 172, 224 S.W. 442 (1920).

Stevens v. Fassett, 27 Maine 266 (1847).

Stevenson v. Board of Education, 426 F. 2d 1154 (5th Cir. 1970).

Stone v. Arizona Highway Commission, 93 Ariz. 384, 381 P. 2d 107 (1963).

Stoner v. California, 376 U.S. 483 (1964).

Stromberg v. French, 60 N.D. 750, 236 N.W. 477 (1931).

Suits v. Glover, 260 Ala. 449, 71 So. 2d 49 (1954).

Sullivan v. Houston Independent School District, 307 F.S. 1328 (S.D. Tex. 1969).

Swann v. Charlotte-Mecklenburg Board of Education, 300 F.S. 1358 (W.D. N.C. 1969).

Swartley v. Seattle School District, 70 Wash. 2d 17, 421 P. 2d 1009 (1966).

Sweitzer v. Fisher, 172 Iowa 266, 154 N.W. 465 (1915).

Szabo v. Pennsylvania R. Co., 132 N.J.L. 331, 40 A. 2d 562 (1945).

Tabor v. Scobee, 254 S.W. 2d 474 (Ky. 1951).

Talmage v. Smith, 101 Mich. 370, 59 N.W. 656 (1894).

Tannenbaum v. Board of Education, 22 A.D. 924, 255 N.Y.S. 2d 522 (1964).

Tanton v. McKenney, 226 Mich. 245, 197 N.W. 510 (1924).

Taylor v. Kelvin, 121 N.J.L. 142, 1 A. 2d 433 (1938).

Taylor v. Oakland Scavenger Co., 17 Cal. 2d 594, 110 p. 2d 1044 (1941).

Teall v. City of Cudahy, 60 Cal. 2d 431, 34 Cal. Rptr. 869, 386 P. 2d 493 (1963).

Tennessee Secondary School Athletic Association v. Cox, 221 Tenn. 164, 425 S.W. 2d 794 (1967).

Thoma v. Tracy Motor Sales, 360 Mich. 434, 104 N.W. 2d 360 (1960).

Thomason v. State, 43 S.W. 1013 (Tex. Crim. App. 1898).

Thompson v. Fox, 326 Pa. 209, 192 A. 107 (1937).

Tinker v. Des Moines Independent Community School District, 393 U.S. 503 (1969).

Tinkham v. Kole, 252 Iowa 1303, 110 N.W. 2d 258 (1961).

Tinkler v. Richter, 295 Mich. 396, 295 N.W. 201 (1940).

Titus v. Lindberg, 49 N.J. 66, 228 A. 2d 65 (1967).

Traynor v. Seiloff, 62 Minn. 420, 64 N.W. 915 (1895).

Trustees of Schools v. People ex rel. Van Allen, 87 Ill. 303 (1877).

Turner v. Caddo Parish School Board, 252 La. 810, 214 So. 2d 153 (1968).

Tymkowicz v. San Jose Unified School District, 151 Cal. App. 2d 517, 312 P. 2d 388 (1957).

United States v. Blok, 188 F. 2d 1019 (D.C. Cir. 1951).

United States v. Small, 297 F.S. 582 (D. Mass. 1969).

Valentine v. Independent School District, 191 Iowa 1100, 183 N.W. 434 (1921).

Van Allen v. McCleary, 27 Misc. 2d 81, 211 N.Y.S. 2d 501 (1961).

Vendrell v. School District, 233 Ore. 1, 376 P. 2d 406 (1962).

Woodsmall v. Mt. Diablo Unified School District, 188 Cal. App. 2d 262, 10 Cal. Rptr. 447 (1961).

Woodyard v. Barnett, 335 Mich. 352, 56 N.W. 2d 214 (1953).

Woody v. Burns, 188 So. 2d 56 (Fla. App. 1966).

Wooster v. Sunderland, 27 Cal. App. 51, 148 P. 959 (1915).

World Publishing Co. v. Mullen, 43 Neb. 126, 61 N.W. 108 (1894).

Wright v. Arcade School District, 230 Cal. App. 2d 272, 40 Cal. Rptr. 812 (1964).

Wright v. City of San Bernardino High School District, 121 Cal. App. 2d 342, 263 P. 2d 25 (1953).

Wright v. DeWitt School District, 238 Ark. 906, 385 S.W. 2d 644 (1965).

Wulff v. Inhabitants of Wakefield, 221 Mass. 427, 109 N.E. 358 (1915).

Yoo v. Moynihan, 28 Conn. Supp. 375, 262 A. 2d 814 (1969).

Zachry v. Brown, 299 F.S. 1360 (N.D. Ala., S.D. 1967).

Zanders v. Louisiana State Board of Education, 281 F.S. 747 (W.D. La. 1968).

Zanley v. Hyde, 208 Mich. 96, 175 N.W. 261 (1919).

Ziegler v. Santa Cruz City High School District, 193 Cal. App. 2d 200, 13 Cal. Rptr. 912 (1961).

Zoski v. Gaines, 271 Mich. 1, 260 N.W. 99 (1935).

Zucker v. Panitz, 299 F.S. 102 (S.D.N.Y. 1969).

Zuckerberg v. Munzer, 277 A.D. 1061, 100 N.Y.S. 2d 910 (1950).